The Seeking Heart

The Seeking Heart

The Prayer Journal of Mae Yoho Ward

edited by Don Ward

CBP Press
St. Louis, Missouri

Library of Congress Cataloging in Publication Data
Ward, Mae Yoho
The Seeking Heart
1. Ward, Mae Yoho. 2. Christian Church (Disciples of Christ)—Biography.
3. Church officers—United States—Biography. 4. Prayers. I. Title.
BX7343.W37A37   1985   242   84-23836

ISBN: 0-8272-3420-1

Manufactured in the United States of America

Contents

Let this book be dedicated to all those Mae loved, be-friended, and influenced, whose lives have been forever changed by the multitude of gifts she so selflessly gave.

Foreword

It is said that many saints dwell among us unknown and unsung. We are the poorer because of our blindness. Yet, when a saint appears among us in a clear and recognizable form, we are doubly blessed. We are graced with a glimpse of the holy in human form.

Mae Yoho Ward was such a person—a woman who endured more heartache than most, a woman who knew physical pain all too well and who was beset with doubts, both personal and theological. Yet she gave herself to a search for faith and committed herself to God. She struggled all the way to maintain balance, but she grew in stature and became one of the esteemed church leaders of our time. Her story is one of importance to all who seek to live *in* the world but not *of* it, to those who would strive for reconciliation, for a better understanding of the meaning of stewardship and wholeness, and for discipline in the spiritual life.

Mae often said, "There are many paths, but only one God." This book is, therefore, not a blueprint to be followed by others. The ways of her life were unique. What you will find here are the simple words and insights of one who used the language to probe inward and beyond, so that our days, no matter how numbered, may be filled with hope and understanding.

One last personal word: Mae, I owe my very existence to you. You gave me life. Then you gave me your life to share. Now you have given unexpectedly one last time. You have permitted me to walk with you across the years of joy and sorrow. You have shown by example what is possible, and you have provided a light to illuminate what lies ahead.

You have given *all. Gracias, mi madre.*

Vaya con Dios,

Don Jeff

1907—Mae (standing) at age 7 with Dee, her younger sister. (Wheeling, West Virginia)

1

Mae

Mae always winced at introductions, for their length grew as her years of service to the church increased. Nevertheless, there were biographical facts of which she was proud, and there were some she preferred to put behind her.

Mae was not an aberration. Far from it. This highly intelligent, industrious, generous woman was a refinement of generations that had exhibited similar traits. In 1737, six generations earlier, her ancestors had sailed from the Netherlands and, with only five shillings, had acquired 254 acres of farmland in Virginia. Within three generations, their holdings were more than 1,000 acres. "We industrious Dutch," she would say with pride.

Margaret Mae and her younger sister, Dee, were raised primarily by their father, a dynamic Christian minister of Lincolnesque stature and oratorical speech. He was to complete his life as minister of Madison Avenue Christian Church in Huntington, West Virginia.

Commitment to causes came naturally to this family. Indelibly etched in Mae's memory was a picture of her father standing on the porch of the parsonage before a lynch mob, a torch in one hand and an open Bible in the other, giving no ground on the subject of prohibition. The conviction and power of his position that night sent the crowd away, and it never threatened his family or church again.

Mae remembered her father in 1919, when she was 19, climbing out of the car with the admonition, "A woman these days should know how to drive." Off she went down the street, the first woman in the town to drive a motorcar. Her pride in that accomplishment and, later, her recognition of her father's progressive thinking concerning the role of women, would strengthen and support her in many difficult and isolating experiences.

After graduating from Bethany College in 1923, Mae became Director of Religious Education for the Christian Church in West Virginia and Ohio. Thus began her long career in association with the Christian Church (Disciples of Christ).

Mae's father had graduated from the Divinity School of Yale University, and she too wished to enroll there. Because she was a woman, she was denied admission. However, she was accepted in the Graduate School of Education and from there enrolled in classes at the Divinity School. Characteristically, she chose as the subject of her Master's thesis *Self-Analysis as an Educational Means for Character Development*. After graduation from Yale in 1928, she and her husband, Norm Ward, also a Yale graduate, served for six years as missionaries in Buenos Aires, Argentina.

It was during this decade that two personal tragedies changed and reshaped her life, causing her to question life's purpose. Because of them she would come to understand pain and loss firsthand and would forever relate to human need and suffering in a new way.

The first was the sudden death of her two-year-old daughter, Dee, in a diphtheria epidemic that swept Argentina. The second tragedy was a painful divorce and the resulting loss of identity as she was separated not only from her husband but also from the small-town pastorate in Wadsworth, Ohio that they served following their term as missionaries.

With a young son to provide for, she moved from state to state, from one menial job to another, from hotel chambermaid to baking and distributing biscuit samples in supermarket aisles. For this highly educated woman, with successful foreign experience, it was a time of humiliation, hopelessness, and near poverty. It was against this backdrop that what seemed to her a miracle, an answer to her prayers, took place. In 1941, Robert Hopkins, President of the United Christian Missionary Society, with headquarters in Indianapolis, offered her the position of Executive Secretary for Latin America.

Thus began the career that many people know as a life of committed service to the church. Within the Indianapolis community of Christian Church leaders, her administrative skills were honed under the tutelage of Cy Yocum, E. K. Higdon, H. B. McCormick, and Dale Fiers. She became Chairman of the World Division and then Vice President of U.C.M.S., serving until 1967. During this long period, she threw herself into the Civil Rights movement in Mississippi and the Farm Workers strike in California. She was awarded three honorary doctorates and authored numerous books and articles. For three decades she was the most sought-after speaker in the Christian Church (Disciples of Christ). As an unapologetic ecumenist, she served at every opportunity in the cause of Christian unity.

When Mae officially retired she joined the staff of the denomination's Board of Higher Education and worked there with great enthusiasm until she "retired" a second time at the age of 76. Then began her active "outdoor ministry" as grounds keeper and gardener for Missions Building, the denominational headquarters. With failing eyesight at the age of 81, Mae felt it was time to take up a new life at Foxwood Springs Living Center near Kansas City, a facility of the National Benevolent Association.

No sooner had she unpacked at Foxwood Springs than she began teaching conversational Spanish. She put in a landscaped patio that was a thing of beauty. Typical of her style was her decision to know the first name of every resident in her building by the end of the first year. At each noon meal she sat at a different table, making friends, hearing concerns, and putting herself in a position to support and help her neighbors. That was vintage Mae Ward, and that is why she continued to grow as she did.

It had always been that way. It was the attitude that I remember so well growing up, for our home was a haven of hospitality. If a State Department official, a missionary on furlough, a foreign diplomat, or a new member of Downey Avenue Christian Church came to visit, they were treated to a simple, predictable meal of pot roast, potatoes, green beans, and of course an evening of stimulating talk on a wide range of issues. The fortunate ones were included in the table games in which Mae showed her keen mind and her predeliction for always winning in a gracious manner. My youth was spent in that environment, absorbing what was said, being invited to contribute, and always being heard and taken seriously.

She was a contemporary of some of Christendom's greatest prophets, teachers, and healers: Kagawa, Martin Niemoeller, Albert Schweitzer, Gandhi, and Martin Luther King, Jr. As a student of history, she was greatly influenced by their lives.

Mae Yoho Ward's life reads like a "Who's Who." But we who knew her do not remember her for her public life. Indeed, it was her ability to dissociate herself from external, worldly things that made her unique.

First and foremost, she was a woman defined by a multitude of relationships:

To her *God,* as her words will attest.

To her *church* she was known as a powerful speaker, a teller of stories of love, sacrifice, and giving that brought the world to our church pews and compassion to our hearts.

To *colleagues* she was a valued sounding board, one whose perceptions were uncanny in the way they cut through superfluous rhetoric and parochial politics.

To *Latin America missionaries* she was a friend, an ally, an advocate who spoke the language and knew the field. She gave of time and energy for them, and her prodigious correspondence shrunk the miles and made the problems manageable.

To *seminary students* she stood as a model of cultured perceptiveness and enlightened thinking, of versatility and success, especially to the young women she befriended and counselled.

To *service staff and secretaries* she was "Mae," a caring person who recognized their contributions and affirmed their dignity. She was a friend who brought home-baked cookies on May Day. It was her typical way of celebrating, by giving rather than receiving.

To *neighbors* her house was the immaculate little pink house with the weedless lawn. She was the good Samaritan who had time to pitch in and help out, no matter how dirty the job. To the children growing up in the neighborhood, she was the best at "Kick the Can" and could outrun any boy on the block.

To *friends* she was a confidante and family mediator. Since she would not gossip, she was often chosen to hear problems and help to clarify values. Hers was a theology of hope, and hundreds would depart from her with a direction that would enhance their own lives as well as those persons they were to serve.

To *family* she was a benefactor, a giver of strength, a companion to grandchildren during foreign travel, a light in the window, and hot tapioca on the stove.

To her *son* she was, first of all, a friend, a mentor extraordinaire, a sensitive, articulate traveller with whom he journeyed through Latin America and through hundreds of books read aloud. She was an eager correspondent, whose weekly letters informed, encouraged, and challenged. She was a scholar who met new ideas without fear and could debate all sides of an issue for the sake of better understanding.

Mae was a model for others who walked in humility, continued to be inquisitive, and lived without fear of what the world might do to her. She was stubborn in her convictions, disciplined in her worship, and strong in her faith. She was one of those rare persons who strove to pray without ceasing and whose life thus became a prayer.

"We are responsible," Mae would say, "to use every day, in every way, all that God has given us."

To that, and to her life, we can only add "Amen."

✳

2

"I'll Keep Trying, God, Have Patience with Me . . ."

My wife and I sat in Mae's apartment, just days after her sudden death. Stunned and looking at each other in utter disbelief, we saw before us the effort of years. We had known of Mae's disciplined devotional reading. Her "Letters to God," posted daily, had been shared many times and had provided a basis for lively theological discussions. But we were still not prepared for this. Here were diaries, meditations, personal devotions, prayers of petition and intercession, and hymns of her own composition that dated as far back as 1927. Here also were twenty-three volumes of detailed writings done between 1977 and 1983. In addition, there were numerous books of recorded dreams, countless study books with margin notations, and outlines for workshops she had led or intended to lead.

We sat in silence, reading and crying, sharing her life, and feeling our loss anew. Then a sense of conviction and direction swept over us, and elation set sorrow aside!

Mae would be embarrassed if she knew her humble letters were to find wider circulation, but she would be pleased if her pilgrimage might help others find what she sought so fervently. This, then, is a compilation of her very candid correspondence with God. We have edited out and destroyed the hundreds of references that dealt with personal and professional problems brought to her by friends and colleagues, and the names of individuals for whom she prayed.

Of over 2,500 letters addressed to God, only a sample are presented here. We have limited the scope of the letters to focus on a time of life that was most challenging and difficult for her. These are the years of transition, of retreat, of resignation and diminishing strength, of relocation and ruptured relationships.

This is the time of life, ahead for all of us, when faith and fear wage a silent war for our souls, when the meaning of death becomes defined so as to limit or expand our future. So it is important to be aware of the primary questions, explicit and implied, that Mae kept before her and presented to God in those last searching years.

"Now that I must leave my house of so many years, how can I, with so little time left, make a new home?

"In moving, must lifelong friendships be affected, even forfeited?

"Is this new place and this new population capable of becoming a caring community? What is my responsibility in this? What should be my strategy?

"What is the relationship of aging to being perceived as 'old'? How can I handle the awful, limiting stereotypes?

"This eternally young me that looks so old to others . . . must it always be 'who I really am' versus 'how I look'?

"How do I deal with pain? Can it be redemptive, even creative? But when the body will not allow it, how do I cope? Must my feeble body make me emotionally frail?

"How does the reality of pain condition the practice of prayer?

"Can I be truly alive if incapacitated, or worse, paralyzed? Can God want that for me? To what end? To what purpose?

"How does my acceptance of death modify the inevitability of dying?

"Now that I have dared to ask, why do I receive so few answers?"

Mae was fully aware that her experience was not unique, that we all share the same journey, no different in kind from any other's. But she was convinced that, in God, the difference could be found that would ultimately give meaning to living and dying. In short, she bet her life on eternity.

The personal salutation "Dear God" is rather recent. It was not used on a regular basis until 1977. Early on, Mae addressed the

Divine with the more traditional "Our Heavenly Father," and correspondingly her communication was more formal. Then came a period when "Creator God" was used. As the years passed and her spiritual life deepened, she became uncomfortable with these more stilted, less personal salutations. Knowing Mae, I can imagine the following conversation:

Mae: (beginning to write her devotions) "Our Heavenly Father . . ."

God: (interrupting) Do we have to be so formal? After all, we've been friends for over seventy years.

Mae: I guess, but I thought You preferred it that way.

God: Not really, but I do understand it. All of those thousands of prayers beginning with "Our Father, who art . . *Mae:* All right, then, we'll do it differently. And by the way, you can call me "Mae." All my friends do.

God: Good. Then you can just call me "God."

Mae: (beginning again) "Dear God . . ."

Here we can see that Mae begins to feel God's presence manifest in a powerful new way.

At the same time, she became sensitized to the place of women in society and saw the need to examine sexist language within the church. The use of "God," without gender designation, was very satisfying to her. Mae's God was never too small, for she was always pushing back the boundaries of possibility and understanding. As she approached God more in a more familiar attitude, she began to go back through her favorite, often-used devotional books and hymnals, crossing out "Thee" and "Thou" and writing in the more personal "You" and "Your."

It was at this point, in following her spiritual pilgrimage, that I became aware of the impact of her father in her life. A minister of great power and compassion, he wrote her every day of her college life; for in the early 1920's, college was a period of monumental transition for a young woman. His letters offered a rich, hopeful theology spiced with practical advice. "Dear Dad," she responded regularly and in kind. Their affection, respect, and admiration grew and bloomed, giving her the assurance of love and respect throughout her lifetime.

"Dear God" also bespeaks an intensely personal, accepting, two-way relationship: unconditional love given in a time of transition. She was, one feels, preparing to return home.

In a very practical way this daily communication was essential. It forced Mae, in her failing eyesight, pain and dizziness, to live in and focus on the present. In her words, "We have to take it one day at a time, in faith and trust, for a brighter tomorrow."

This, then, is the very private journey of Mae Ward. A unique human being who rebelled and rejoiced, she was more dialogue than dichotomy. This was the way she lived—with intensity, probing the possibilities, fussing at her fears, fuming at her failures. She was a woman who felt ego to be a fault, yet whose personality could not help dominating; who feared flattery, yet who found in it feedback essential for her effectiveness.

Mae was a person who wanted answers but did not want to be told; whose theology fervently embraced free will, yet who longed for a father to safeguard her future; whose candid perplexity, and at times anxiety, over not having an encounter with the Christ was offset by a direct, loving relationship with God. Perhaps she was not different from most of us—just more honest.

Mae saw in the smallest events opportunities for service. For her, contacts with people provided occasions for prayer. She sought high things in lowly places. The image of her wearing gardening gloves and carrying a basket and a rake was a fitting one, for she swept up and took unto herself the litter and autumn leaves of countless persons. "God asks no more of us than that we act where we stand," she would say. Then, in an enthusiastic and slightly impatient tone, would add, "Let's go to it!" And so we shall, letting Mae speak for herself. We would ask only that you handle these letters with humility and compassion, for we are, in a real way, eavesdropping on the murmurings of a saint conversing with her God.

*

The Year Ends; The Year Begins

by Mae Yoho Ward

The year rushed by
    Laughing, crying as it went,
    Filled with moments of every hue.
Not always did the colors fit the tapestry
    I was weaving for my hall of memories.
Now it is finished, ready for hanging.
    Look, it is beautiful.
The somber hues weave in and out
    Among the sunshine yellows and bright reds.
The warp and woof are strong and true.
    I dare to call it "good."
The new year rushes at me pell-mell.
    I hope for serenity of soul,
    For moments of contentment and peace.
Another tapestry will be woven,
    Its uniqueness will be the history of the year.
A task lies before me—
    To weave each moment into the fabric
    Making it strong and true
    To intertwine each color, that the pattern
    May blend into beauty.
I pray when the year ends
    And another tapestry brightens the hall of memories
I may, with honesty, say, "It is good."

3

A Preface to the Letters

A Word About the Format and Arrangement

Each of Mae's letters followed a form that seldom varied, except in the case of illness or travel, which forced brevity.

First, there was the familiar "Dear God." Then she would often relate a concern or event of the previous day or night and would lay out her itinerary for the day ahead. Next, she would comment about her efforts at writing, relating feelings of success, failure, or satisfaction with the discipline. A litany of thanksgiving usually followed, often including original poetry or hymns. Then there were prayers of intercession for the family, friends, church workers, and world leaders, in that order. These were usually very specific regarding needs and problems. Suggestions or solutions were never imposed. "Your will be done" is implicit throughout.

The next major area was that of faith and theology. Mae was concerned more with making pointed observations and raising personal questions than in formulating positions and intellectualizing. The latter she had done with gusto during her public life of investigation, study, and teaching.

Another major theme was that of health, death, and the future. This usually constituted about one-third of the letter. It was here that she became most candid.

In concluding a letter, Mae usually turned optimistic, punctuating the final paragraph with insightful little quips, phrases from her reading, or a final word of thanks, appreciation, or love. The signature was always "Mae."

In excerpting these letters, we have not tried to follow her exact format. In some cases, a complete letter will be found as it was written, but most are a distillation and combination of letters. They are presented in chronological order, beginning in 1977 and concluding with a final entry shortly before her death in 1983.

A Word About Mae's Daily Written Prayers

Most days, Mae wrote a short prayer on the blank page opposite the printed prayers in John Baillie's *A Diary of Private Prayer.*

For seven consecutive years, she would make an entry on the same day and comment on the prayers of the preceding years. When the book was filled, she bought another copy of the same book and began the process again. At the completion of the second book, she had fourteen years to examine. We found three full books of the same edition, spanning twenty-one years of prayer and reflection!

There may have been other such books that were lost or destroyed. We will never know.

A Word About Mae's Reading of Books

Mae was a prodigious and eclectic reader. Even when operations for cataracts and a detached retina brought great pain and lengthy recovery periods, she allocated some time each day to read with the aid of high-intensity lamps.

She never ceased being a learner. She was an exceptional teacher because she was a diligent student. Not only did she do extensive research for her own presentations and publications, but she also reviewed and critiqued the sermons and manuscripts of others.

From examining these letters to God, we know that certain books, out of hundreds read, were especially valued during the years 1977—1983. These are noted for the reader's interest. Those which Mae claimed were most helpful, because they gave new insights for her ongoing spiritual journey, are starred: *Becoming A Guest of the Holy*, by Harold Johnson (Christian Board of

Publication 1978), *The Christian Understanding of God, by Nels Ferre (Greenwood, 1979), Creative Dislocations, by Robert McAfee Brown (Abingdon, 1980), *Dimensions of Prayer, by Douglas V. Steere (Harper & Row, 1963), God's Kingdom Has No End, (Christian Board of Publication, Meditations of the Heart, by Howard Thurman (Friends United, 1976), The Other Generation Gap: The Middle Aged and Their Aging Parents, by Stephen Z. Cohen and Bruce M. Gans (New Century, 1978), *Rolling Thunder, by Doug Boyd (Dell, 1976), *Sitting By My Laughing Fire, by Ruth Bell Graham (Word Books, 1977), The Search for Silence, by Elizabeth O'Conner (Word Books, 1979), A Season with the Savior: Meditations on Mark, by Edward R. Sims (Seabury, 1979), The Third Wave, by Alvin Toffler (Morrow, 1980), To Kiss the Joy, by Robert Raines (Abingdon, 1983), Waiting for the Morning Train: An American Boyhood, by Bruce Catton, *Wishful Thinking: A Theological ABC, by Frederick Beuchner (Harper & Row, 1973), Women, Change and the Church, by Nancy Van Scoyoc (Abingdon, 1980).

✱

1917—Mae's high school graduation picture and that of her father, Jeff W. Yoho. (Huntington, West Virginia)

1941—Mae's first publicity photo, when she joined the staff of the United Christian Missionary Society as Executive Secretary for Latin America and the Caribbean. (Indianapolis, Indiana)

22

4

1977—1978

"Does the future look promising to you? What are your expectations? What, as Creator, do You hope to see happen? Come and let us reason together about shaping the future."

May, 1977

I opened the envelope which had been slipped under my door. As I held it, I knew I had never before had a note like this one. Even the paper felt different and it seemed to give off a light. I was eager to open it and yet, I hesitated, speculating on the writer, After turning it over and hunting for a postmark, which wasn't there, I tore it open and read,

"Mae, you have now retired. You have many times said, 'I am going to really, truly take time for God each day,' and off and on you have done so, but it has been more off than on. Your time is now yours. You may do what you decide to do. This is an invitation to meet me each day. I look forward to our time together.

Hopefully,

God"

I accept the invitation, God!

Gratefully,

Mae

Dear God,

Thank You, thank You, thank You. The whole world rejoices with the sunshine! Help me to present You with truth this day. It is audacious, I know, but I will try.

I should like these pages not to be a prayer in the usual way, but a voicing of my thoughts—as much a conversation with a friend as is possible. Often, I know, it will fall into petition. Often, it will be a quote from something I have just heard. It will be like a letter to You, God, telling of my happenings and thoughts. I know You know, but You have asked us to talk to You, to share with You, to pray to You. Be patient, please as I begin.

You know best about the gardening job at the building.* Life is too full to start it now, but I do want it, God. I will leave it to You.

Should I accept the writing assignment for *The Disciple?*** I like being asked, believing in that way people still think, "I'm with it." I need that, but accepting for ego satisfaction is, if not wrong, at least not enough. Do I have *anything to say?* If I have, can I say it well? Will You give me the message?

My mind flies out in many directions as I think of those I love and add my petition for grace for each one. May the letters I will write from this day forward be "grace-notes."

God, I must write about fear. I have it. I am ashamed of it. The devotional today said, "Fight fear. Fight it as you would a plague. Fight it in my name." I belong in Your goodness. You have helped me through many difficult situations. Why do I act so awful now? I want to be able to trust You absolutely, to face each day with joy and praise. I want to say firmly, I will *not* fear. But my will is so weak when discomfort hits me, or when I think of exiting from this life. It's going to come, so of what value is fear? None, so I will place my hand on the imaginary book of Fear and say, "I will not stay here."

I am so grateful to you for so much, so many blessings are mine, that life seems almost too good to be true.

Mae

★ ★ ★

---

*Missions Building, national office building of the Christian Church (Disciples of Christ, located across Ohmer street from Mae's home.
**National magazine of the Christian Church (Disciples of Christ).

Dear God,

How beautiful is your creation! Put it into the hearts of millions today to worship. May the joy of our faith shout forth!

The days go by so quickly. The outdoors grows so fast I can't keep up with all the pruning. Thank You for the strength I am given, that I can go and trim bushes for an hour and a half. Help me to organize my time and my energy.

Now, especially, I ask for help at the retreat. Keep me humble and in close touch with You, God. It's so strange how when I try to think of You and study the Scriptures, a thousand other things run through my mind, like ironing the piece on the back of the chair, sending a card, washing the clothes to wear at the retreat and getting gas for the car. How, God, do I capture my butterfly mind in a net of meditation?

As I read the devotional material of the saints, there is so much more struggle and pain than joy and peace. They are more sensitive people than most of us, but still, Lord, it seems they have an over-supply of a sense of sin. But then, I too have guilt feelings. I have them because people think I am so good when I am not. I love doing things with and for people, but I'm not unselfish about it. Forgive me.

Thank You for my eyesight. Do, oh God, let Bill have eyesight too. I feel at times that I would like to command certain things, but I am not You.

As I remember now my friends and loved ones and write each name, I pray that this day may be blessed for . . .*

Remind me, God, that I will *never* have more time for loving, caring, and forgiving than I have right now.

Mae

★ ★ ★

---

*We found prayer lists of hundreds and hundreds of names, people for whom Mae petitioned each day. Lists changed and names were dropped, added, or repeated as her "prayer partners'" needs for healing, support, or reconciliation were resolved. It appears that, on the average, eight or ten people per day were thus remembered, but it was not unusual to find twenty, thirty, or more names. There is a deep sense of assurance in finding one's name here.

Dear God,

I am an original.
I am one-of-a-kind.
I am a combination of
   traits,
      abilities,
         skills,
Unlike any other in the world.
I bring together in my personhood
   experiences,
      loves,
         dreams,
            ambitions,
               and anxieties,
Which equal no other's anywhere.

What, therefore, is demanded of me,
A one-of-a-kind person?

As an original piece of pottery
Gives delight to all who see, touch and use it,
So shall I stand out, giving
   joy to all who see,
   touch and use me.
That's a lot to ask of me, God.
It is so easy to fail!
Still, I have been given
   my own unique opportunities
   to live a fully crafted life.

And so, forgetting the failures of the past,
And remembering the Creator
Who made me one-of-a-kind,
   I will be exceedingly glad for today,
   and be a giver of love,
   and be a "bringer of beauty."

So I hope and pray!

Mae

Dear God,

I look forward to these moments when I can write You. Are You looking over my shoulder, or don't You need to because You know it all anyway? The devotional I read just now said, "Share all with You as a child shares its joys and sorrows with its mother." That is exactly what I intend to do.

Why do I have such blockage in calling You "Father"? I think it is because my concept of You has grown. I cannot confine You to a Father image. Yet that is the way Jesus said to address You. For You to have a Son would in some way imply the help of another person—a female person. If such is not necessary in the spirit world, then You could as logically be called Mother since it is the female who gives birth. I have not been able to believe that Mary was a virgin. Should I believe that, Lord? Is that important? Anyway, thank You for Your *parental* love and caring.

Help me to choose the priority for my life right now. Here I am, retired, and yet, God, there are so many things to think about and get done—the garden, the Building, the luncheons, the worship committees, the house, the Quadrennial,* packing for the lake. Help me, God as all of these fall into place.

Other's illnesses make me realize how perilous is each day and uncertain the outcomes of each action. Living in faith is the *only* way to live, yet my mind continues to ponder what I should do about the future. Am I unwise to keep on staying alone, to think I can go on being useful for many more years? God, you know the turmoil I get into so often. Help me to trust You. Do make known Your will for me, so that I may know what is best.

Oh, God, I do so panic when there is a sign of trouble—the sharp pricks of pain around my heart, the sign of a nose bleed. Thank You that this morning the pain is gone. I did put myself in Your care last night and You cared. Now, as I put my middle finger in the hollow of my throat and, with the beat of my heart, say, "I know that God is with me" several times, become relaxed. Thank You, God, for this evidence of Your presence in the flowing of blood through my body.

Strange are my thoughts this morning. Pope John is dead. He seemed so alive . . . but he still lives! Thank You.

Mae

---

*Quadrennial Assembly of Christian Women's Fellowship, held at Purdue University.

Dear God,

I look forward to this time of reading and writing. I should probably just sit and *listen,* but I have been such an activist! I am so grateful to be able to "see," to "read." I have always found "writing" a release for emotions. I should add "listening" to these morning periods.

Studying for the communion service last night was helpful. The Disciple tradition seems so right for remembering Jesus, whose life was so simple and yet, maybe, we have made it so simple we do not recognize the presence of Christ. May I not lead the group into confusion of thought.

God, I find myself so disgusted with people smoking and I must not spend nervous energy that way. Help me to overcome my resentment of their lack of stewardship. It distresses me so that health, so precious, can be so foolishly squandered at such a price to self and loved ones. It must make You sick! You have given us the right to choose. Why do we choose to abuse it so?

In the light of all the big problems of the world, what I write about seems trivial and very personal—but these letters are meant to be personal—You understand that, God. I began it so that I could discipline myself to talk with You. I am ashamed that I have no high and lofty thoughts, but I praise You and ask that all those who have had deaths in their families recently, be able to give thanks on this day, knowing Your love surpasses death.

You have given me another year and it has been good. Continue to help me through whatever days remain. I pray for your guidance and gentle leading through green pastures and still waters and then find myself surprised when it happens. Why is that? Thank You for all the gentle thoughts, cards, cables, and letters from people on my birthday.

I am so pleased to be able to say, "God is in residence."

Mae

★ ★ ★

Dear God,

It is mine to decide that each morning I will sit in "my established place" and read, sing, and write. I belong to many precious supporting groups: Downey Ave.,* Spiritual Companions, Reading Group, The Reading 5, The Prayer Group, the Book Club, the family. Thank You, God, for each of these

*Downey Avenue Christian Church, where Mae held membership.

groups. May I not fail in my love for them. I shall join the prayer group this morning, but, to be honest, I would rather work outdoors and pray for all who pass, as I rejoice in the growth of plants and flowers. Yet I talk so much about prayer, my conscience makes me go.

So many women are getting ready for the Quadrennial. Bless each. May Your Spirit be very evident to all who attend. May we have assurance for our doubts, some strength for our weakness, some vision of our duty.

Thank You that I feel so well, that I could walk a mile in wind and rain without ever becoming tired, that my mind functions. I'm better than I was two years ago due to Your help. Accept my thanks.

Now I would like to make progress, or at least take a step in how to talk with Jesus, how to have Him as a traveling companion who would move with me though the activities of the day. You know my feelings better than I. One thing is sure: I need strength, love and courage from You. Stay with me.

Right now my future looks very unsure. Of course, I cannot live many more years and cancer of the lung may be my exit door, but it seems a hard exit. Many others are facing futures like the one facing me. There is no reason why I should have a special privilege, but I do ask for Your presence.

Mae

P. S. Jerry Falwell was on TV the other day, preaching about homosexuals. God, who are you blessing these days?

★ ★ ★

Dear God,

This cool morning should make me feel ambitious and ready to do tasks about the house, but I only want to go back to bed. I'm disturbed about little things—a rusted fender on the car, having to take money out of the savings account to meet expenses, how to get packages to the post office, and a dish to Evelyn in all this rain. Such little things preoccupy me when I should be praying for the sick, the hungry, those who do not know Christ. But these letters to You, God, were to be about my day—the trivial. Now, having told You everything, I'll try to get on with something more important.

Thank You for the books I am reading. During this week, give me the plan and the thoughts for the retreat. Help me not to panic, but to wait patiently for Your help. Soon a hundred women will arrive with expectations. Please be in our midst. Help me to uplift and inspire. May I do nothing which thwarts Your will and hope for these people. Bless all Christian women and the service they give.

I like creative activities and I tire of "Bible Study," as we do it in the group. I am also unsatisfied (not dissatisfied) with other approaches. Are we enamored with ourselves, as we try out "fantasy trips" and move no closer to You? We need help in knowing how to praise You, even how to receive Your help.

I just read that intercessory prayer was like the bringing of a plant out of the basement and placing it in the sunshine, and the sunshine and light brought the change and growth. So, I bring my family one by one and leave them in the sunshine of Your love. May the Quadrennial committee be in the sunshine today as we plan. May I feel Your power and strength as I stand in the light seeking ways to develop the retreat theme.

Thank you for the youth of Downey Ave. and for their ability. More thanks for the teachers who lead them. Help me to see clearer my task in working with them. Help me to put ego aside and self-satisfaction (an unworthy goal) and help these young people to feel some of the joy I have in my Christian faith.

How can we help the hungry and discouraged? My life is so comfortable and more or less secure and I am so content. I ought to be helping, but how or where? Do I, as some friends say, "have this coming to me," and accept it as "my rightful reward"? My outside world is so beautiful. Help me to make my inside world beautiful in love and service to those in need.

Mae

★ ★ ★

★ ★ ★

Dear God,

This morning I began to ask your blessing on President Carter when a mosquito buzzed around my head. I immediately got up to get some repellent. It may not be an actual mosquito that interrupts my prayer but a task of the day, or an errand to be run can pop into my praying and off I go again. If I consider them prayerfully and in the light of Your will, could my tasks be considered prayers?

I have started reading for the retreats and as I read, I find myself wanting to stop and speak to You about it, wanting You to be a close partner, pointing out the important things, suggesting what I should say and how I should say it. Make it Your message, not Mae Ward's. I need your powerful nudging in my mind so that the time the women give for the retreats will be worthwhile.

I read all of the helpful books of people in whose daily life love shines out and faith exists. In my own life, I feel my expression of love and faith to be so ordinary that they have little or no effect.

I have been trying to think of Mary as she went to the house of John. Where were her other children? Did they all think Jesus had gone off on a tangent and so would have nothing to do with Him? Because Mary stood by Jesus, did they think her foolish and forsake her too? What bitterness for her! In contrast to that gloom, another (beloved) son sends me a lovely April poster. I am so grateful. Please, Father, be with Don Jeff. Give healing for his back. I have written "Father" when something happens within the family, for that is the word which comes to mind. It does not represent "maleness," but "kindness."

Once again, the physical looms large. My body is tired and sore. I pray earnestly for less pain that I may do my work and serve You. I am not a good "witness." I do not sing the song well when I hurt so. At times I am sure You are helping me and then again, I feel You are letting me go on hurting for some reasons known only to You.

The trash pick-up men are going by. May they know that they are engaged in a necessary and helpful task. May they be given strength by day and rest at night. Thank you for the same. Your servant in training,

Mae

31

Dear God,
   I have been sitting quietly, listening, remembering. Do You know the sounds I like best?

   The hello of friends
   The harmony of a great organ
   The steady hum of the engine of my car
   The ringing of the phone at ll:00 on Sunday night when Don Jeff calls

   Raindrops on rustling leaves
   Waves on the shore putting me to sleep
   Deep breathing, after exercise and the beating of my heart
   Singing hymns aloud, when driving alone
   The clinking of ice in a glass of tea on a hot summer day
   The breathing of an audience, captivated by the words of the speaker

   Many and varied are the sounds of Your wondrous world!

   I am reading Raines' book. His book and other things all point to such a possible communion with You that I am envious. I cannot find it. On the other hand, my desire to think, to write to You— and I hope to listen, too—is so strong, that I get up at 6:00 in order to have this time, fearful that if I do not get up, the activities of the day will crowd out this time, which I have come to depend on. I want to let Your grace course through my body and brain. I want to be filled with Your spirit that I may calmly, peacefully, serenely, live this day. May I not let the logistics of living be uppermost.
   It's raining, so I can't work outside today. I shall miss not praying for each one who passes by. Help me to get some inside work done today. Help me to know if I should have guests. Help me to know if I should accept appointments. I am truly confused about the role I should take now. "Give thanks for whatever happens, for this is what God in Christ wills for you." Do I give thanks for dizziness? Does God will it for me? Do You, God? May I know why? I can't remember as I should. Something is wrong. How should I plan for the future? The fact that I do not worry about heaven or hell, but live only one day at a time makes

_____
*Robert Raines, *To Kiss the Joy.* Abingdon, 1983.

me live on the surface, I expect. But it seems so futile to think much of the future. Praising You through all eternity sounds pretty boring, too, and yet praise seems to be the principle ingredient of future living. What are the important or non-important reasons for living? Enough contacts to have life human, enough service to feel helpful, enough health to be able to serve and maintain contact, enough money to live without worry? Always more questions than answers!

I ask Your blessing now on all the activities of my day. It is hard to stay awake, but let not my dullness dull the lustre of the days for others.

Mae

★ ★ ★

Dear God,

I am writing at the close of the day instead of the beginning. A quiet moment didn't seem a part of getting started, but I thought informally about You and others. I said "Thank You" many times. I am inclined to think that *anything* which happens is what You plan. It is such a comfortable way to live.

According to one author, I am not doing the right thing in writing You. The page should be blank. I should empty myself and become as nothing and You would take possession of my soul. But Jesus said, "Make all your requests known," and writing them down somehow clears the day for me. I'm not far enough along in my spiritual journey to become as "nothing." I don't know how to . . . and I guess I don't want to.

I seem so torn between getting the outside work done and the many preparations I need to make for assignments. Thoughts of Crystal Lake* make me long for that place and its sense of quiet and serenity. What is it I should be doing now to regain that spirit? Surely my delight in living and my joy in feeling closer to You should not depend on a *place*. But I do like praying for each one who passes as I work outside. It's a little of the same feeling I have when I garden—that I am working with a Force greater than I. Do I kid myself, God? It's so easy to see Creation taking place in a garden—with people it is much more difficult!

---

*Crystal Lake, Frankfort, Michigan, is a summer community of cottages owned by members of the Christian Church (Disciples of Christ). Mae rented a cottage there from 1942 through 1982.

A Diary of Readings: "God speaketh once, yea twice, yet man perceiveth it not. In a dream, in a vision of the night, when deep sleep falleth upon men in slumberings upon the bed." I haven't thought of You coming to me in my dreams. They seem unrelated events, musings, experiences and thoughts of my own, not Yours. I wish You could speak to me in my dreams. Help me to dream and thus to see.

I did nothing yesterday for any of Your people. Today I will try again, but harder!

✳ ✳ ✳   Mae

Dear God,

It's Sunday morning and I have the prayer at the communion table. For the first time, I'm going without something written.It seems that I need the thrill of the service to know what to say. May the Spirit, which abides within me, offer the prayer. May I "let go and let God."

As I think about my life this morning, I can remember many painful things . . . broken relationships, unhappy times, painful encounters, many hospital experiences with deep anxiety, and yet through all these disasters, I must acknowledge that You have been near me with unusual aids of grace. Now, I near the end of the 7th decade with deep gratitude and thanksgiving. May Your name be praised! The statement that one cannot be ready to "pray on call" keeps coming back to me. The "let me know," certainly sounds as if You are available to help me as a neighbor. Are You? I like to think You are.

Help me, God. I can't understand. I have been to the Convalescent Home. Some who are there are skin and bones in wheel chairs and are lonely. Many are running out of money and need operations. There are scores of others who are in worse shape. Why, God, is it necessary to have people finish life in this fashion?

The church bell has just stopped tolling. May all who hear think of worship this morning. I forget so fast, but now I remember, I did not pray for Bill and Jennifer when the 11:00 whistle blew on Friday. If my callousness can be corrected, I now stop and pray for them.

Now, literally, dozens of names and faces come before me and I am eager to remember them before You . . . the people I have met in retreats . . . all of my "Spiritual Companions" . . . the young folks and the leaders of Downey Avenue Church . . . the

34

friends to whom I write . . . the family. Grace this day, to each and every one.

Love me too,

*** Mae

Dear God,

You know why I didn't write yesterday. Thieves cut the screen and took my purse. I was trying to get ready to leave and all was bedlam. The police came. All day yesterday, in spite of speeches and a good retreat, the "scene of the crime" played in the background. God, it won't be easy to throw off fear. The expense of the "crime" is so financially costly for me. The crime is also costly for those who took my pocketbook. They got so little, really, but they became more skilled in knowing how—getting deeper into that way of life. Be with them. Forgive them. They really know *not* what they do.

Thank You, God, that You drove with me last night. I don't see at all well. Thank You for Your presence. If within the limits of Your laws, You can heal my eye, please do so. I have faith, but I also have a mind that deals with things logically. Yet I do believe Your power can stabilize my sight.

What did I mean last night when I said that I could not die for the principle that Jesus is the Christ? I fear when I doubt. I believe that Jesus is Your son, that he truly showed Your love and showed us what kind of a Heavenly Father You were. But that His death was for *my* sins is hard to believe—that He, of all the people who have died for their convictions, is the one who saves me?! Yet, I have felt a presence, at times, when I have prayed at the communion table. Was it the presence of Christ in our midst?

I'm trying to be unselfish about accepting gifts. It's hard for me to give up any form of independence. Yet I know the value of interdependence. Especially when I think of You, I know I am dependent upon You for everything. This is a fact of life, so help me to be careful of the blessings you so generously give through others. Let me be sensitive to the "ecology of relationships."

I find my thoughts of Dad, Norm, Don Jeff and Jeff all running together in a strange way. The men in my life have such vital ingredients of living. They are so precious and so different. Praise and gratitude are the cornerstones of my life this week. Thank you, God, for everything.

Mae

Dear God,

It's Sunday at Crystal Lake. Thank You for a safe trip and for all going well, even though we are nine persons of varied personalities and ages. Continue to be present. I'm tired physically today. It's strange how being with people takes so much energy. Help me to carry with me the serenity of this place. Thank you for the warm feelings of love that have existed within the family. I sing a song of thanksgiving. May the joy of human togetherness be ours.

You are ever precious, present and gracious. I read a lot of material others have written and realize how far short I fall from the state of spirituality others obtain. I want to rest everything in You—the family, the church, my assignments, my friends, my health, my house, the folks at the Missions Building, everything, God. How can I make progress toward this goal? That is probably the wrong attitude—trying toward "goals" instead of resting in You.

I am back in the "slough of despair" because my blood pressure is so high. What in the world have I done? I was really feeling on top of the world, and Wow, I hit bottom! I write so much about myself and my physical well-being. I'm sorry the "I" looms so large in my life. Help me to think of others and their acute needs and plan how to do something about them.

I look back on my life from my earliest memories to now, and it leaves me with the impression that I have been, (though at certain times I felt bereft), and am now, being guided by Your gracious and loving hand which has made events possible which otherwise would have been impossible.

Thank You for my heritage, as I now remember Dad's death. I think of Grandpa Yoho and Grandma Yoho, of Aunt Alma and her care. I was too thoughtless about all she did for me. There is no way to make up for past neglects. It would be easy to let guilt take over, but I shall give thanks instead.

Today I will pray for each person with whom I come in contact. That is a decision I want to keep, but I realize how hard it will be. Thank you for people to love.

Mae

★ ★ ★

✦ ✦ ✦

Dear God,

It's such a bea-u-ti-ful morning. I love it here. Thank you for this period of time of quietness and thoughtfulness. Truly those who wait on the Lord renew their strength. At least I walk without weariness and I so love this half hour of reading, thinking, praying, writing. In writing, I center my thoughts, but maybe it *would* be better to keep the pages blank and just listen. Or should I do both, write and listen or maybe listen and then write? All the authorities talk so *much* of just "waiting."

The week goes fast—too fast. I feel like the Apostles on the Mountain of Transfiguration. "Lord, it is good to be here. Let's stay," but I must go back to Indianapolis. I love my little home and my friends, but this has been wonderful.

God, I'm afraid of the emotions of people, or I'm more sensitive to them or I dislike anything which upsets the peace of an occasion. Less and less, I like to probe and analyze problems. More and more, I would let the past be the past, and less and less, I worry about the future. All the books say, "Pull out the problems, look at them, decide who is at fault." I would rather let them be. Am I lazy, are they too painful, or do I just trust You more?

Do You remember when he asked if one could have intercessory prayer for a car? And I said, "Yes, I believe You are interested in everything which touches us, even when we are selfish." You may say "No" when the basis is selfishness, but You do hear, and even if the prayer is not granted the way we want it, there has been an answer. But I don't think You say "No." I believe You point out choices!

Young Jeff and I just talked for almost an hour, which was the perfect ending of a perfect day. He is an alert, intelligent, attractive youth. Anybody would feel a sense of pride that such an individual is a part of today's society. So I end as I began. What a blessed day. No human could ask for more!

Mae

Dear God,

Good morning! Isn't it wonderful to feel good? Do You have anything like our physical pain?

This is the last day at Crystal Lake for this year. My gratitude goes beyond words. You must know how I feel. It has been good to have Don Jeff read aloud *Waiting for the Morning Train.** It has been so rewarding to have him, the book, the cottage (and me) all together. As the "late train" comes for me, may I clearly hear the "porter" say, "I'll call for you in the morning." Give us safe travel.

Again, I'm concerned about the physical. Surely old age would not take strength from my muscles this fast. Guide me medically (if that is what is wrong) to the right medications. But, God, may I not call on You for healing? May the Great Physician touch me, make me strong, help me, heal me. Help me to put away my fears about the future. I spend too much time worrying about how life is to end and what plans should be made now. I should either decide to go into a "home," and *go*, or quit using time and energy thinking about it. God, please take over the task and give me some directives. I need help.

. . . .

We are ready to go back to Indianapolis and I pause to converse with You before I go. Thank You for Your mercy and guidance. "Let my soul stand cool and composed." It's going to be hard today, Lord, to be outgoing and cheerful. I'll need a little extra push.

Mae

Build a little fence of trust
    Around today;
Fill the space with loving work
    And therein stay;
Look not through the sheltering bars
    Upon tomorrow;
God will help you bear what comes
    Of joy and sorrow.

From Janet.** Bless her.

---

*Bruce Catton, *Waiting for the Morning Train: An American Boyhood.* Doubleday, 1972.
**Janet Sugioka, a personal friend.

Dear God,

Christmas. How lovely! Let Your grace descend upon us that we may live in peace and love one another.

In my day, an orange was considered a *good* Christmas gift. There was always a silver dollar in the toe of my stocking from Grandmother Yoho. I was fifteen when she died. She had lived with us a year and I missed her. Whenever I think of her, I see her in a black apron, working in the kitchen. She baked dozens of pies for the threshers and put them on the pie shelf which ran along one side of the big kitchen at the farm. The three summers spent at the farm are delightful memories. What a fortunate childhood I had. Thank You, God, for past, present and future.

Help me as I give devotions Wednesday night, entertain tomorrow night and begin preparations for the State Retreat. "I need Thee, Oh, I need Thee. *Every* hour I need Thee." What a wonderful, old hymn that is.

What is prayer? Communion with You, talking and writing to You, listening to You, letting the consciousness that You are in me be evident, enjoying some moments of quiet and thoughtfulness? The Orthodox priest said, "When you pray, don't theologize." Another says, "Requests give authenticity to your concern and love." It's evident from these letters I make plenty of those.

My heart overflows because of my constant blessings— Downey Avenue, loving friends, good health, this crisp and beautiful day, a son that cares, a warm, comfortable home, enough money for a good living. And on this day, I offer special thanks for your Son who cared and for Your love, my God.

I love You, too.

Mae

✳

5

1979

"Keep me from feeling that financial security is so important. I am far too conscious of it, and yet, God, I hope You do not find it necessary to take it away, so that I learn to depend on You alone!"

Dear God,
    When I looked back a year to see what we talked about, there was no record, there was *no* day. It gave me a funny feeling. "Leap Year" offers an extra gift of a day! Should I use it in a special way?
    It's unbelievable what this time of talking to You has come to mean. The fifteen minutes have stretched into half an hour or more. Writing this brief note to You is such a help. I like to tell others about the habit and how it can brighten the day. Let me do it without feeling pious or giving that impression. What I feel is delight and companionship and it's hard to convey that.
    How much good does it do for me to think of and mention the names of people to You? I do not know *Your* response, but I know *I* frequently try to answer the prayer by doing some simple thing for them. My mind and affection go racing from one name to another, craving a blessing for each. You know every one of them. . . .
    I have been to the Regional Retreat of the CWF, so I've spent a lot of time trying to lead people. Whatever I did wrong, help me to forget. Whatever it was that encouraged, help me to remember. They are a great group of Your servants. Be with them when they

are discouraged. Help each of us to be more committed because of this experience with Your word and in Your presence.

God, let me talk with You about the fainting condition, and please, give me some guidance. I have not had it once since coming back, until last night. There had been constant talk, and again the pressure of "no solitude" got to me. How would going into a home help me in that situation? How do I avoid the feeling of hurry, hurry that comes with the slightest hint of meeting a deadline? There will be many people here in the next few weeks, and I find myself jittery, almost fearful about the amount of work. Dear Lord, help me to take one day at a time, to make each event count for You and them. Be in this home with such force that all realize Your presence.

In Your care,

Mae

P.S. It's *still* snowing and it's beautiful, but we surely don't need it.

★ ★ ★

Dear God,
Let Your grace fall upon me that I may live in peace and love others.

Let your grace fall
As hot water in the shower
On a cold winter night.

Let Your grace fall
As soothing lotion
On my rough, chapped hands.

Let Your grace fall
As the sunshine
Pouring through the window
After days of January greyness.

Let Your grace fall!

You are in the blowing snow.
Here, in my warm room, are You.

Your loving care is everywhere,
You are in the concern of Lambrini's phone call.

You are in my mind, urging me to remember all,
You are present in every loving heart.

Every place and always Your loving care surrounds us,
And we rejoiced in Your everlasting love!

✷ ✷ ✷

Mae

Dear God,

How are You this morning? Busy looking after all of us?

Thank you that I feel so well—so much better than other winters—is it because I walk, take vitamins, have work, write You each day? Perhaps it is because of all of these.

As I look back across the years, I feel my experience in Vanderbilt, in the class with Nels Ferre, helped me to move to another stage, a so-called higher stage. You became *very* personal. I felt I could approach You as a dear friend and yet as Creator who sincerely had my "good at heart." You might refuse my requests either for my own good or the good of others, but You would always give them consideration. A year ago, I turned my written petitions into "Letters to God." I did not envision how that would help me "center-in" each morning on the day and its happenings, how much easier it would become to have a running conversation or at least speaking-to-You throughout the entire day.

Thank You so much for being with me at the communion table yesterday and for the idea of the "cup of salvation" and the "cup of service"and our commitment to use both, to preach the Good News and to help people in the nourishment of the physical and spiritual . . . the importance of both brought together in that symbol. Thank You, God, for an idea I had never had or ever heard expressed.

You know what a problem I have understanding who Christ is and what He means in my life. A very few times in my life I have felt close to Him, as Lord. There is no problem in thinking of You as God, as Father God. Loving and giving daily prayer for You provide so often in so many ways. I can only think of Christ as

Savior because He let us know You. Help me, in spite of myself, to accept and understand Jesus as Lord and Savior.

A year ago, I was asking You about the future. You have given me a great year—free from serious illness, enjoying my own home, with opportunities for work. Deep thanks for this past year. Help me to trust You this coming year regardless of the events.

Thank you that the bad fall I had on the ice did nothing serious—only a swelling on the back of the head. My guardian angel must be very alert!

So many blessings. Like a child, I am still never satisfied.

★ ★ ★

Mae

Dear God,

What a wonderful night of sleep and rest. What a wonderful opportunity to write the worship program. What a wonderful thought that a place is reserved for me in Heaven. Help me to continue to develop that theme for others—and to live, myself, so that I am worthy of it.

I sit here looking out the window and see the grounds and think of all the work to be done. Help me to realize what poison ivy is and help me find something to get rid of it. Why does the outdoors need poison ivy, God?

Can I really use my work at the Missions Building in Your cause? Does a prayer for each person passing by do anything for that person, or only keep me in touch with You? Help me to make my prayers for those who pass effective.

Yesterday, my eyes were so troublesome! When they are, it is hard to be with people. If there is any way in which I can help my eyes . . . . Most of all, help me to live above this discomfort and live today with joy and peace—found in the fact that You are a God who cares. I want so much to have faith, to believe that what I ask will be granted, but I remember Jesus' praying and yet having to say, "Your will, not mine, be done." How does having faith and praying that prayer fit together? Should I be praying so much for myself? At times I think my letters to You are too full of "I" and "me." Yet I need Your cleansing power, and writing You about "me" helps to clarify certain thoughts and attitudes. I'm working hard to pray without ceasing, but if the minutes I spend could be put in a computer, they would be shockingly few, I fear. Stay with me, I'll keep trying.

A long list of people appear in my letter a year ago. All of them still need You today, but I mention a few especially . . . *

The visitor asked the old Quaker, "Dare a person speak here?" "Only if you can improve the silence." Help me to remember that today.

★ ★ ★   Mae

Dear God,

The sun shines on the grass, so very green. It sparkles with dew-diamonds. Thank You that my house guests were so happy. I wanted the work at the Building and now that I have it, I wonder. I wanted work, but not responsibility. Be with me. I want to put my head back and close my eyes and let You guide my thoughts, but I know my inertia leads me, not to meditation, but to sleepiness. Shame!

How shall I fill this day wisely? Time rushes at me and I put up my hands saying, "Wait, wait, I am not ready for the Bible study, not ready for the retreat, not ready for teaching the class, not ready to start a garden. Wait, please wait. I must read a great deal. I must write letters. I must make phone calls. I must be quiet and ponder." But Time, you will not wait.

So, today, I am . . .

a bundle of fears about the future

a bundle of nerves wanting a tranquilizer

a lump of clay longing to be molded

a spirit housed in a deteriorating body

a fisherman trying to catch tiny darting ideas in a net of many opportunities

a car caught in a snowdrift of laziness, spinning my wheels and getting noplace

burdened by the programs I must write

a squirrel scampering here and there in search of truth

a cat falling asleep when I mean to pray

a runner in the Marathon of Life, not eager to stay running until I reach the finish line

a human being, trying to be a Christian.

How confused I am about life, and You, and Your presence and Your guidance. I feel You are near, and then I wonder if that is my imagination. Am I just "whistling in the dark"? I read and sing about taking no thought for the morrow, and then worry about getting the steps fixed!

---

*Eighteen persons are listed, with the special reason that prayer is needed noted by each name.

Dear God,

Last year I told You of my gratitude for life and its blessings. This year it is even deeper. I have finished reading and singing and now feel like facing the day. I got up feeling disgusted with myself and resentful toward You. I had prayed for sleep and freedom from pain and received neither. Now I feel You answered prayer with a wonderful visit and three beautiful carnations from a friend.

"Guide Me, Oh Thou Great Jehovah." I learned that hymn in the sixth grade. The language is not for children of that age and now is far from contemporary. Still, the lines come to mind often and the opening sentence is my prayer, "Guide Me, Oh Thou Great Jehovah."

I keep reading about being "open in prayer" with You. It seems to me I am, God. I don't see how anything could be hidden from You! You know how I like to succeed, what ego satisfaction I get in helping people, how selfish I am, how stingy, how dependent upon financial security, how reluctant to accept leadership, how critical of people whose opinions are different from mine, how proud, how little humility I have. Stay with me, God, but don't make learning new ways too painful.

God, I take no credit for remembering people in prayer and their recovery, but I want to thank You for what You have done for those I prayed for a year ago . . . .

As I go to the retreat, show me how to make the hours of help and inspiration for each. May no one leave without some blessing. Help me to realize every minute that my strength comes from You. I would earnestly ask also that I can go through the time without too much physical weakness and dizziness. Should an 80-year-old be doing this? (It's a little late to be asking, isn't it?) I don't like the way I have become conscious of every action and word, in order that I not show my age. It's silly, but I am conscious of it. Do not let spontaneity slip from my spirit or joy fade from my heart!

Be with me as I lead the devotions at Group One tonight. Now I must see about food for that meeting. Have a good day.

Mae

★ ★ ★

Dear God,

Another birthday. Why do I dislike them so when there is nothing I can do about them? It's interesting that I have felt this way since I was 34. Silly, isn't it?

A year ago, I wrote, "Thank You for Frances and Lambrini, both of whom are so good for me, and to me." I say the same again this year, only more so!

Do I try to do too much in this period of each day? Should I just sit quietly, trying to empty my mind, trying to be a guest of the Holy? Give me some nudges, God, as to the way I should spend this time each morning. I am so grateful for it, even though I may not use it in the best way. Guide me, please.

Bless the people who were under this roof last night. I wrote before of the "tyranny of intimacy," and when I am away from the intimacy of friends, I delight in the fact that nobody can call me. At the same time, I delight to hear their voices and life would lose much of its value if not for them. Last night I received two compliments and they were so encouraging. Help me to remember to say things which strengthen people.

Every Friday at 11:00, the whistles in Indianapolis blow, but how many people know why? On the 11th day of the 11th month at 11:00, the armistice papers were signed. That was "the war to end all wars." But we go on planning for war. It is as though the souls of men are restless until they can make the weapon which will destroy everything. How well I remember that day when bells rang and whistles blew. We rushed out of the high school building to form a spontaneous parade and march downtown. Practically every girl in school had a navy middy blouse from some sailor. Mine had come from a guy without a family, that Dad had given a room to when he was on furlough. The future was *so sure* that day. The future was bright. Every fellow coming home was a hero and life was going to be good for all. God, was "the war to end all wars" just the beginning of the final chapter of "The War That Will End All Peace"?

Prayerfully,

Mae

★ ★ ★

★ ★ ★

Dear God,

I am so glad I finally developed a habit which adds so much to life—this habit of writing You in the quiet of the morning. But, the nights are *so* strange. Buoyancy of spirit flies away and puzzlement takes its place. In what form and when will death come? Since I can't know, I should cease to think of it. But thoughts seem to overpower and make me sleepless. So many of my peers are ill and suffering. It's clear I am not certain, that I find it hard to trust. What can I do about this, God? I want to trust and in the clear light of day, I seem to.

What *does* come after this life? Am I so casual about the final judgment that I don't believe it will happen? I do feel people will be given another chance, because, being human, I would do that, and You are greater. I think You would give me a passing grade for "effort," though not for "accomplishment." I hate to face the fact that it is too easy for me to put words into others' mouths— what I think they would have said "if given the chance." I should be writing books and then it would be OK to "develop the characters." Forgive me my sins, but, God, it doesn't always appear to me as sin! Until it does, I will probably go on.

May Your presence be known to the maintenance men at the Building. There are so many executives and staff who need to stay in close touch with You. Those that pass me each day as I work on my knees in the flower beds, for each I offer a prayer. I notice them at the windows. Are they watching me, God? Lead them, each and every one, in Your way. May they understand what it truly means to be "called."

I am going to church now to lead the worship for the retired clergy. I think You have given me something worthwhile. Help me to remember it was *You* who gave it. I am but the voice.

My heart overflows with gratitude. Like a school child, I want to write on the blackboard a hundred times,"Thank You, God." As the day goes on, may I see the blessedness in every person I meet. May every contact provide the opportunity to share joy and provide a blessing.

Mae

Dear God,

I am so eager to make this part of the day "a thoughtful, prayerful time," that I try to pack it too full. Yet, I find it helpful to follow a series of activities: reading, singing, praying, writing. Will the Spirit within help me to sort out what is important and set the tempo for this? Thank you for the minutes, for the reading material, for the hymnbook, pencil, and paper, for ideas, thoughts, and dreams.

Yesterday was such a good, satisfying day. I got up too late this morning to have the feeling of calm for things ahead. Slothfulness is not usually a part of my vocabulary and it must not be a part of my life. What do I need to bring before you at this moment? The well-being of each woman here! As she goes home to meet the family, to take up the duties of laundry and cooking and getting along with others, may some of the unhurriedness of these days stay with her. May the experience have deepened my determination to be "Your guest." Thank You.

God, I am intellectually so sure of You. I long for some emotional sign of Your presence. Thank You that these times of quiet are so meaningful to me, but help me to know how to get on with the true discovery of You. I sing so fervently of Your faithfulness, of being surrounded by Your care. This I believe, but I fear the future so. I believe You will go with me into a nursing home and be with me during a terminal illness, but I dread it. I am frightened by the thought. I see these people in nursing homes and feel so sorry for them, and spend too much time imagining myself in one and hating it. Help me to live one day at a time rejoicing in whatever amount of Your love I can envision. You know how absurd it is for anybody to think of me as a "saint."

Give to me Your forgiveness and love. Thank You for rescuing me from my many acts of carelessness.

Mae

* * *

Dear God,

Let's chat.

It's Saturday night and I'm home from the retreat. Thank You for all the women and the way they took part. Bless each one tonight, back in the grind and working hard to build a relationship with You. May I free my schedule to write many of them and express my gratitude.

Last night a woman said, "There were miracles all along our way," referring to their trip in Florida. I know what she meant. Everything seems touched with God when I think of it. From turning on the engine of the car, to safe traveling, to finding needed things, to ideas that come, to freedom from pain. When I am thoughtful about it, I can feel the joy and the excitement which come from knowing You touch my life.

Thank You for the expression of love and affection of people. May I be worthy of them. God, I feel at times that I *am* able to radiate *Your* love.

Last year on this day, instead of requests, I offered thanksgiving. I would do the same this year. Thanks for all the organizations of goodwill and especially for the UN, which, in spite of conflicting ideas, continues to try to bring peace. Thank You for all organizations of beauty, especially the museums of art, and for all people who support them. Thank You for all religious organizations, especially the local churches, communities of faith, which make a place of hope a reality. Thank You for all affirmative, loving human relationships, especially for the family and the good letters of yesterday. Thank You for a cozy home, in which I can extend hospitality and kindness. Thank You for a body and mind which function and which can be instruments of Your grace. Keep Dree and Jeff in the hollow of Your hand. Help the whole family (me, too, of course) to be worthy of Your love.

As I was taking my exercises before bed, I suddenly, strongly, felt, "I want to live forever." So many times I have said,"I'm ready at any time (for death)," but last night, I felt so good, life was so precious, that I didn't want it to end. Thank You for that amount of "peace which passes understanding," which is mine.

Mae

★ ★ ★

Dear God,

God, I have faith and confidence in You, but I do not have faith to believe that I know how to ask. However, I go on. Maybe I will learn. You know my thoughts this moment, the future overpowers me at times. I try to trust You and throw them off, but they remain, too often, dark blots of frightening uncertainty. Plainly, I'm wearing out. I long to be able to trust You fully for the future. The idea of being kept alive when death is at hand has a shattering effect on me. I wish and hope and pray for confidence that you will see me through, without a deterioration of personality. You live in me. Let Yourself always show.

The past years I have lamented the fact that I did not have the certainty of the born-again-Christians. I have prayed for the healing touch of Jesus. This morning, I think that I have been touched, not in a dramatic way, but in a persistent, subtle working of mind and body which enables me to go on hopefully, day after day, rendering some service. I'm not a born-again-Christian, but a Christian-being-born.

I am so governed by weather, that it is sad. 90 degree heat makes me feel wasted and horrid. So many millions live in it constantly. I am ashamed of myself. Help me to live above such bodily discomfort. As I used the electric clippers, I thought *I* am like the electric clippers: an instrument which can be used for cutting out unworthiness and pruning for beauty. But I, like the clippers, have no power of my own. To be of value, I have to be plugged in and recharged. I find these minutes with You, doing that very thing. In a way, it is like a miracle and yet it is probably as pragmatic and down to earth as attaching the electric clippers into the outlet. I try to plug into Your power and wisdom and something happens—the current enters me. Give me enough charge, God, that I can keep "clipping" away all the rest of my days.

Accept my intercessory prayers, Lord, by which I try to help others. Most of the time, I doubt that my prayers can or should be answered, because I am not wise enough to know what is good for family and friends. But may my prayers be open to Your sight . . . .

Thank you for the beauty of this time of year and for the way plants grow. How similar are our lives to the lives of the world in general. Spring flowers are like youth, with vigor and beauty, but aren't the fall leaves pretty? They are, but they do not excite us as do the spring flowers.

Love in the autumn,

Mae

★ ★ ★

Dear God,

For three days I have not written. That is the longest I have gone since I started these morning prayer letters. It would be easy to drop a habit I thought was well established. Help me, Lord, to be faithful. I feel pretty miserable this morning. I feel rushed . . . to the doctor, to the store, to clean the patio, to attend a luncheon, to get dinner for guests. They can all fall quietly into place if I just take them one at a time, but right now my desire is to go back to bed and keep my eyes shut. During these moments, calm me down. Help me think of others and, Oh, do be with me during the coming week.

Let your grace fall on me. Last night I was so arrogant. It's a wonder that anybody tolerates me, to say nothing of loving me. I'll try again, God. After all these years, I should have learned, but I haven't. The worst of it is, I try to justify my behaviors. As far back as I can remember, I have been too sure of myself. The "Big I" is still a major part of my repertoire! There is some nasty little demon here that needs to be put in his place.

Put "thought seeds" in my mind about the chapel. Help me not to be peeved because I accepted it, but guide me to say something of meaning about Your love.

I wonder. How did Jesus deal with physical pains and aches? I've never thought of Him having anything wrong, not even a headache. How did He deal with these? Thousands, if not millions, are in more pain than I am, so I pray for them. May medicine be available and may You be there to heal. I, too, ask for Your healing power tonight. I long for sleep, but the pain dominates. Give me your grace to accept this night and praise for the measure of well-being I have.

I can see how my eyesight is an "instrument of His glory," but not my sightlessness! I have been reading about the close connection between body, mind and soul, and how they influence each other. The mind has the power to energize the body, but cannot the body, with its illness, overpower the mind? I am shameless when it comes to asking for healing—but I so clearly remember Dr. McCormick when I was going in for the breast operation. He came to the house to tell me the prayer *was* answered, and I need *not* fear. He was right!

Gratefully,

Mae

Dear God,

Here I am at the lake. The beauty and calm of this place creeps into my soul. I am so grateful for the chance to be here again. The sun shining through the trees makes shadows and spots and streaks of light that never fail to delight me.

Thank You, thank You, thank You, that You are, that You care, that I am able to think of You so many times each day, that I do often feel You are in control of my life, and that I am tossed here and there by fate. When I feel such direct guidance, I want to tell others about it, to pass it on. Show me how to do that without their thinking I'm a little crazy!

Thank You for a wonderful night of sleep and interesting dreams. If death is like sleep, then death is wonderful—it refreshes, renews, adds an extra dimension. I had such a real dream about Jesus and Jeff. Jeff was driving my car, Jesus was in the front seat and I was in the back.

Mae: "Jesus, isn't my grandson a great guy and a delightful person?"

Jesus: "I have been observing him all of his 19 years."

Mae: "Me, too, and it has been delightful watching him develop."

Jesus: "I have watched, too."

Mae: "Aren't you pleased?"

Jesus: "He is a fine young man!"

Mae: "I know!"

The same is true for Your Son, God. Aren't we lucky?

I need help, God, to understand what the death of Jesus means. Paul's letters are full of salvation only through Him. That He told us about You and made clear Your power, help, and love, I understand and gratefully accept, but that His death had anything to do with my sins, I find hard to believe. Help, Thou, my unbelief.

What should I be doing today to magnify Your name?

Mae

★ ★ ★

Dear God,

What are the central ingredients of prayer? How about:
Meditation, thinking of You (I do a minimum of this)
Contemplation, resting in You (I do some of this)
Conversation, speaking to You (I do a lot of this)

All together they make up prayer. Thank You, God, that You are within me.

I now have two weeks alone. I have so much time for meditation, thought, prayer, contemplation. May it be a time of renewal, a time when Your Spirit, living within me, can take over and make my personality in tune with Yours. I delight at seeing the sun filter through the birches, but when I try to use them as the object of meditation, I want to fall asleep. I fall so short in quiet times. I do a better job of relating to You when I dedicate my activities to You.

I realize how hard it must be for people to have meditation time when they live in households. I know how much it means to me when I can quietly bring the coming events of each day to You. I love it here in the quiet of the morning, sitting on the porch swing. I marvel again and again how I, Mae Ward, am permitted this joy when millions never have any of it.

Thank you for the relationship with Jeff. Help me to be as understanding as he is, but help me also to have patience when many are around and help me to not worry about money. I find myself doing what Mother did, writing down again and again the list of food needs for the month, adding it up and having a deficit. I thought she should not worry for she had *me*. *I* should not worry for I have *You*. The statement, "Those who wait for the Lord renew their strength," is certainly true. It has been so already this morning. Thirty minutes is never long enough anymore, for there is joy and renewal in this period.

God, I must point out to You my anxiety about my left eye. Each morning I awake almost afraid that there will be less vision than the day before. You know that reading has become almost impossible—even figuring out accounts is difficult. God, I do cry out to You, and most earnestly, that I may be allowed to keep my vision 'til death. Are You leading me as the sight goes from my eye, God? I am so much more worried than I thought I would be. Do stay close beside and help. Touch my eye, touch my spirit. Help me to trust Your goodness. It is so easy to trust when all goes well. I am so jittery when it doesn't. May I say well what I should tomorrow at church. With my eyes so bad, I am so fearful. God, if I am not to see, help me to accept it and let it not destroy my faith.

Mae

53

Dear God,

I'm in the last week at Crystal. Thank You for the wonderful place, for freedom from the "tyranny of intimacy." It's strange how I need friends, how I appreciate people's concern for me and how glad I am to be free of anybody worrying about me. It's all a part of living in tension. Help me to pray more often for others. May I go through this day without criticism. May I use my mind and will to dispel any prejudice I meet today. Keep me from arrogance and, if it comes, help me to keep it out of my voice. May I be eager to listen to anyone in trouble or difficulty and pray Your healing power for them. May I be able to stay in touch with You all day. I know every breath I take is indication of Your power and love. May I be worthy of it.

As I read about the future, all of the resources of the earth will finally be gone. Maybe that is the way life here will cease. It looks as if hard times are ahead for the next generation. I cannot take that in, my mind says "yes" and then rebels, saying, "Something will happen to change it." Could it be that Jesus would return "in a cloud of glory"? My mind has a tendency to laugh that off. That doesn't seem in keeping with the way You do things, but Jesus said it would be that way. How much of the New Testament can we take for fact?

God, I keep trying to understand Your love with the awful things which happen to people—long months of illness in particular. Illness seems to me especially bad, the illness that precedes death. How do I have "perfect peace that casts out fear"? I have a horror that having talked of Your love and its dependability, I will have some experience that will deprive me of that certainty. Sort of the feeling Paul had "after having preached, I will find myself a castaway." Why am I so afraid of pain? When I think of the physical sufferings of others, I immediately think of myself, saying, "What if that happened to me? How could I take it?" I want to be concerned about the others and not myself. I *don't* like my attitude. I am like a child who thinks she is earning the approval of the parent by being good and whose first priority is *approval*. I think if "I am a good little girl, He will look after me." My attitude is so child-like. There is comfort in the admonition of Jesus to "become as little children." Little children *do trust* a loving father. I, too, shall try.

Mae

Dear God,

My left eye is even worse today. God, is all eyesight going to go? The New Testament tells of people who touched Jesus and were healed. I have been praying for Him to touch me, for Him to take the initiative. Maybe I should do the reaching out. If so, how do I do it? I listen to the born-again-Christians talk. They are so sure Jesus came into their lives and changed everything. They are *so sure.* I am *so unsure,* that I have the presence of the Lord in my life. I can use the simple words they use, "Come, Lord Jesus," but I feel no particular awakening. Where or what do I do now? About You, I do feel a relationship. If I could trust Dad, I have a certainty about trusting the great, compassionate God, the Father of us all.

The activities of the day will give the opportunity to show love and consideration to all I meet. But, before I go, I bring into the warmth of Your love, the following . . . [24 people are mentioned].
. . . .

Thank You for this nice, cool evening, and the laughing fire in the fireplace. It is so pleasant to be here. The past years I have been leaving Crystal about this time. How grateful I am for the past five summers spent here. Each one seems to get better. I dare to ask for another one, if I am able, but right now, my deepest thanks.

Mae

6

1980

"I go kicking and squealing into old age. I probably entered life the same way."

Dear God,

Another year and I am still struggling with the way I can contact and have a close relationship with Jesus. Could it be that basically I am afraid of that relationship? Is it because I see Jesus as a *person*, not as the *Lord?* At any rate, have patience and help me to grow in understanding.

I don't understand the Beatitudes, yet I am going to try to talk about them tomorrow. The "poor in spirit," must be acknowledging one's ignorance, one's need to learn. I have no trouble accepting this idea. "Those who mourn"—this comes a bit clearer if it means sorry for past sins. "The meek"— strength without braggadocio, no need to fight, to even raise one's voice because one has the Right.

Will your Kingdom ever come? With all the violence in the world and the belief that problems can be settled by guns, the Kingdom is like a dream. What part can the Church play? Enough questions.

I give thanks that You have guided and helped me through retreats and programs of all kinds. More lie ahead and I pray for Your help as I teach tomorrow, lead devotions at Group One, present the book *The Culture of Narcissism,** lead the Ivy Club program. Then coming up Monday is the Trustees meeting . . .

---

*Christopher Lasch, *The Culture of Narcissism.* Norton, 1979.

when will it ever end? (I know the answer and wish I didn't.) I am grateful for sound mind and adequate body. By the way, I don't think I like what last night's dream has to tell me. I was on a big ship. We stopped so people could swim. I went off by myself. When I joined the group again, I bragged about how far I had swum, but I had not been in the water! (The "plunge" has never been easy for me. God, at least help me to keep getting my feet wet!)

You know about these all too human problems, but now I add an additional ounce of concern in praying for . . . .

Thank You for the blessed fact of my experience.

Mae

★ ★ ★

Dear God,

Here it is night again. I prayed on the way to the store and back, but I am missing the sweet communion I have with You when I use half an hour in the morning. At night, I feel so sleepy. It just doesn't seem like the right time of day to have a tryst with You.

Thank You most gratefully for this comfortable house. Do please help me to know when I ought to leave it. I have never felt more keenly the need for Your guidance in this course of my life. The talk with Don Jeff about Foxwood Springs makes me think all the more of it. I really want to stay right here. Can You give me some sign, please?

This morning I left the TV on and heard an evangelist telling how You chastise us with pain, problems and loneliness. That is impossible for me to believe. Yet, a year ago today, I was struggling with the same problem. I know and expect a variety of hardships to be a part of living, but I cannot believe You send them. That You help us through them, that You turn them to advantage, *that* I can believe, but a loving God Loves, and Love is kind and patient.

I am so conscious of the physical. Far too much of my concern is for the pains of my body and what the outcome will be. I wish for the ability, strength and will to turn my body over to You knowing that whatever is possible (with an aging body), You will do. The pain is back again this year and I have so little patience with it. Are You trying to teach me patience, or only that I am mortal? What should I learn from this? Certainly it puts me more in tune with friends suffering from cancer. I'm glad I do not fear death, but the entrance to death, I do fear.

Should I accept responsibility for a group at the Quadrennial?
It's not good to get a reputation for prayer!
Bless this day to the good of all.

Mae

★ ★ ★

Dear God,
The sciatica is so bad I am home from church. Why do I write You every day? What is it that urges me on to write? I pray that the "urge" is the spirit of the Lord within me, joining our petitions together.

Why do I pray? Because so many of my friends are ill and I am helpless to do anything for them, so I turn to You.

Why do I pray? Because I am so thankful and grateful. "My cup runneth over." I look back over my progress of the years and can see how many times You came to the rescue—for others, for me. No one in my situation could be so callous as to fail to give thanks.

Why do I pray? Because You hear me. Because You understand what an odd creature I am. So "full of good works" and yet so selfish, so eager to be of use and yet so self-centered. It helps that knowing all about me, you still listen.

Why do I pray? Because I cannot help it!

Give to all of us some of the faith and hope that must have been true of the early Christians. The Graham book is so helpful. "Don't crowd me. I need room to grow, to stretch my wings, breathe deep and slow, to look about, to think things through. Don't hem me in, don't block the view."* May I go forth, God, free to show Your love to the world.

Thank You for sleep. Thank You for sunshine. Thank You for health. Thank You for President Carter's efforts toward peace in the Middle East. Thank You for people who write gracious letters.

Mil gracias por toda la bondard que recibo en echo dia.

Mae

★ ★ ★

Dear God,
I'm excited about this daily tryst and want to tell people, but I don't want to turn them off because I seem to be "far out." But my life has been a bit "far out," or at least a "reaching out" to new experiences. The devotional book suggested to complete a 9-sentence biography. Here is what I wrote.

---

*Ruth Bell Graham, Sitting By My Laughing Fire. Word Books, 1977, p. 141.

58

1. *I am fearful.* I try, but cannot eliminate, completely, my fear of how difficult the last of life can be.

2. *I am joyful.* This joy comes from my delight in God and the people I love.

3. *I am selfish,* and unselfish, often at the same time. I decide to give, then consider the amount, and sometimes reduce it, thinking of my own needs.

4. *I am proud.* Proud of my background, my parents, Don Jeff and his accomplishments, and the grandchildren. Proud of the work I have done and even now do. Proud in the wrong way, too— that I am not eager for the material things, but am satisfied with a simple house, clothes, etc., in a greater degree than some of my colleagues.

5. *I am critical,* and yet naive. If I go to a meeting that has a good feel and spirit, I say, "That's great." If I hear a lecture or a teacher, I take each idea and logically decide if it is true.

6. *I am stubborn* and brash in an argument with my peers, but with my superiors, I sometimes relinquish a position, thinking I do not know enough to contend with them.

7. *I am sensitive* and can empathize with those with whom I am involved.

8. *I am a debtor* to great causes which have given me great opportunities to go beyond myself. I was present at the organizing session of the NCC,* the organizing session of the CWF, the third and fourth assemblies of the World Council of Churches, when we began to see the need and power of the Third World. I was in the first contingent of twelve Catholics, Jews and Protestants to go to California to talk with Chavez and throw our weight behind the grape pickers. I went to Mississippi to register blacks. I was Vice President of the DOM** of the NCC. I served on the Theological Education Committee of the National Council of Churches when the emphasis was training nationals to teach because it was more important than building buildings. I am a debtor, indeed, to great causes that forced and invited me to think, grow and participate.

9. *I am in love* with a son who has made a child-parent relationship beautiful, and I am dependent upon his love.

How blessed I have been. Thank You.

Mae

---

*National Council of Churches
**Division of Overseas Ministries

Dear God,

Today I just want to sit quietly, trying to put my life in perspective and wash out, erase my resentment at having to try to "be in style." I hated being cold last night, having to wear a skirt because I didn't want others to disapprove. "Do not worry about what you shall wear or how you will be clothed," but I do. I buy a suit and waver between keeping it or returning it. I don't really care about new clothes. Help me to deal with this rather insignificant problem.

Last night we went to see *On Golden Pond.* Some movies have made me cry, others have made me indignant, some have inspired me and others have made me laugh. But when this was over, I was content. Maybe age has a lot to do with it, because Hepburn and Fonda are not young. They are such marvelous models of "aged people." Love came through so genuine, so down-to-earth, so clean cut, so tender. Most of all tender. It had the element Don spoke of in his last letter. "Jenny will come back (from the store) with 20-30 lbs. of groceries in her backpack and I like to have dinner on so she can take a nap. We do live well together in interdependence! In this place, and in all we've shared, It's good to count fully on one another." Life has an abundance of blessings and high on the list is "count fully on one another." I love to have people around, but living alone I have never found distasteful. Rarely do I feel lonely when living alone. When I do, I write a letter. The somebody who will read it is a human contact. When the letter is to Don Jeff, I am conversing with him. As I write, I see him reading, and I know what some of his reactions will be. I feel that way about You, too, God. It's "good to count fully on one another." Thanks to *On Golden Pond,* and all our letters, I have a deeper appreciation of LOVE.

How grateful I am for this "Pink House." It has been a haven in more ways than one. I wonder how many people have been entertained here and for the most part had a happy experience. They must run into the thousands.

Give me directives as to how I should plan for the future. Does the sweet letter from Tom Johns at Foxwood Springs mean anything special?

The problems of the world are so overwhelming that I limit my prayers today to my own small circle . . . .

. . . .

The phone rang and I didn't get back, but I have been in touch with You *many* times today.   Mae

★ ★ ★

Dear God,

Good morning! "Thy presence through the day, I pray." The night was long, sleepless and restless. Since my spiritual health is so closely bound with my physical, I'll need help today.

God, do my actions and words really reflect You? I want to be sincere and genuine, but You know my inner doubts. I talk of the uniqueness of each person as a joy and then want to change them to conform to *my* way. Forgive my pettiness.

This morning it has become clearer that prayer to Jesus Christ, the Lord, is appropriate. That He and You are "at home" in me. That You can feel comfortable, "at home in me," as guests can feel "at home in my house." If You are at home here, then You cannot be ignored. Three meals come around regularly and the people in the house have to be reminded, and remembering brings action.

Can I pray (as I want to), "Gentle Jesus, let Your grace descend upon me," or should I pray, "Christ, who brings a sword, pierce my soul"? Basically, I don't like violence and personally, I feel "grace" is a more desirable characteristic.

Thank You for all the wonderful women of the CWBM* and their concern for the mission of the world. Thank You for the hundreds who have remembered me with cards and messages. Let Your love be felt by each this morning.

How remarkable it has been that there is always some task to do. The history survey is completed. The gardening will be over shortly. What is ahead for this winter? Should it be entertaining? Getting people's minds off their work and relaxing with games? Should it be letter-writing and trying to be an "amplifier of hope"? Should I accept more retreats and assignments, spend more time in intercession? You have led me in the past, lead on!

Mae

*Christian Women's Board of Missions

61

Dear God,
>
> It is Easter
> The Lord is risen
> The Lord is risen, indeed
> Thank you!

This is a beautiful Sunday morning with the Spring bringing all the magic of resurrection and new birth. Thank You for the warmth of the sun and the expectation of the spirit. Be with all who preach, teach and sing, that You may be glorified.

The beauty of the world is beyond words.

The green freshness of the grass
The happy yellow of daffodils
The forsythia making banks of gold
The vividness of bright red tulips
All of these delight the eye and lift the spirit.

I lift my eyes from earth, to see,
Flowering magnolia trees
Tulip trees bursting with flower
Each bud trying to out-hurry the others
The soft greenness of new leaves on every tree
Every place I look is beauty
And over all is fragrance.

★ ★ ★

★ ★ ★

To some extent, this happens to my soul. Here, too, is newness, hope and grace.

How graceful are the seasons. With what delight I greet each one. How fortunate I am to be alive this Spring.

Oh, God, I thank Thee for each
    sight of beauty that Thy hand doth give,
For sunny skies and air and light
Oh, God, I thank Thee that I live.

New memories each returning May,
    hover around me while I pray
    and help me this and every day,
    to live more nearly as I say,
Thy will be done.

May the family be well physically, but more important may their spirit be in tune with Your will. What I pray for them, I, too, request.

We share with You and Your Son this joyous day.

Mae

Dear God,

I'm 80. That sounds awful and yet the difference from when I was 70 is so little. I'm a bit more in touch with You daily, for which I am so grateful. During the decade I feared I would lose my sight, but I do see. *Seeing* is a wonderful blessing. Thank You. I puzzle over the fact that health is mine and friends are dying. I keep reminding myself such a fate is in store for me. I have also selfishly prayed that I won't have these long months of inactivity. If there is anything I should be doing to stay well until You are ready for me, show me. Thank You that during this decade Dree and Jeff have grown into such fine young people.

I told the doctor yesterday that my blessings far outweigh the problems of the years and she asked me what pulled me through. I said, "God did. How else could I have managed?" When I have prayed to die, You have not granted it, but you have given me what it takes to go through it all. Was I too optimistic when I talked to her? Did I act as if my life were a success story? Well, in a way it has been, thanks to the gifts and opportunities You have provided. Still, I have to do something about birthdays, I mean my attitude. I have deepened my dislike of them and have acted so petty. I don't think I can change my dislike of the silly celebrations, but I can act more courteously, and I will. I don't shudder at being 80, but I shudder at, "My word, she is 80," or "For 80 she does very well." It is horrid not to be what you *are,* but what others think you *should be.*

In spite of my blessings, life pushes me on. By eight o'clock, two phone calls changed my plans for today and tomorrow. It seems there is so much, when all I want to do is work outside and read the contest manuscripts. "The world is too much with us . . . . We lay waste our powers," and yet what powers do I have left to lay waste? Let your grace remain with me all day as it gets hot and I tend to get hurried.

You know I am grateful. You have given me another wonderful year! Your goodness follows me "all the days of my life." Prayers offered last year have been answered. Now I remember before You . . . [fourteen names are mentioned]

Sweeten now the relationships in this house. Enfold us in Your unconditional love. Have a wonderful day!

Mae

★ ★ ★

Dear God,

Thank You for this beautiful Sunday morning. Go with us as we go to Louisville. Help each one of the panel make a worthy and effective presentation in Your name. May Your favor fall on the family, scattered across the country. Thank You for the maturity of Dree and Jeff and for the excellent youth they are. Continue to bless them and help them to acknowledge Your blessing.

Did You enjoy the dialogue between "Me" and "I" yesterday? There was a joint decision to mow the lawn. The temperature was in the eighties and the humidity higher. The front yard got mowed. It was mostly in the shade. Then we went to the back yard with all the sun. After a few turns, the conversation began:

I: Gee, this is hard work.

Me: You are right. Why don't we quit?

I: I want to get it done.

Me: There's another day and if not, it won't make any difference.

I: There will be another day, all right, and it may be hotter.

Me: OK, go ahead if you insist.

I: But I really don't want to. I hate doing it.

Me: Why do you hate it and still keep on?

I: I hate knowing that my strength gets less and less and the work harder and harder.

Me: Well, you are 80.

I: Yes, but people 80 win races and perform all kinds of fantastic feats.

Me: Apparently, you aren't one of them.

I: I know, and that hurts. I want to "die with my boots on."

Me: If you keep up this mowing, you may do just that.

I: Look at the water running down my face. Gosh, but I'm tired.

Me: Let's go inside and have some of that lemonade we mixed up.

I: OK, I give up. But doesn't this tell us something about going to Foxwood?

Me: I've known for a long time that we should go, but you are so stubborn.

I: I'm getting closer to it. Besides, wherever we are, I'll have to point up the realities.

I'm glad You understand and accept me!   Mae

★ ★ ★

Dear God,
Today, I start to Michigan. Go with me every step, every mile.

. . . .

Thank You. I arrived safely without blacking out. Now I am here at Crystal with everything so wonderfully quiet. Let me make the very most of the many advantages You make possible for me. Guide me to use this time with joy and relaxation.

There is a haze on the lake, but the sun is slowly dissolving it. How beautiful is this world. How calm the lake. How peaceful my own spirit. Yet there is always the fly in the ointment. Today it is dozens of small specks flying before my left eye. Now and then an arrow glides across my vision. The retina must have tiny tears in it, letting in the light. Be Thou my vision and guide me through the cloudiness of my days. Jesus said to the blind man, "What would you have me do for you?" He said, "Restore my sight." Jesus said, "Go your way. Your faith has made you well." God, how, oh how, does one have that kind of faith? I believe in answered prayer, but my prayers must be too feeble. I do not know how to make them strong, how to get the result the blind man had. "Go your way. Your faith has made you well." I pray again.

The four of us sat around the dining room table for an hour after lunch, talking about how we felt and what we believed about prayer and God as Creator of a universe. When we had finished, we had settled nothing. We were left with one sure word:"Why?" As I have often thought, I can and do at times doubt *everything*. But, invariably, I come back to what, for me, is a fundamental principle of my life—that it is possible to establish a relationship with You! In some absolutely unprovable fashion, communication does exist between the Creator and the created. So it is that I will continue to pray.

If I dare ask for Your help, I must confess the pettiness of my own spirit. I am ashamed of how much I want people to think well of me and appreciate me. Help me to put down my own ego in favor of Your ruling my life. At the same time, I feel You want me to be proud, happy, full of zest—that You do not want a milk-toast person. Help me to know how to "mature" and yet retain enthusiasm for life.

Mae

Dear God,

The day is perfect, overcast though it is. I am at peace listening to the waves lapping against the shore with a slight, refreshing breeze blowing in from the lake, like a caress on my face. The wild wheat across the road sweeps gracefully back and forth at the touch of the wind. My offer of gratitude for life, health and these few minutes of communion. Sitting outside the Riley's cottage, feeling the coolness, hearing the voices of children, having friends here, enjoying the evening with the neighbors, having serious conversations with Jeff, getting letters from family, remembering friends, all add up to contentment.

May I always remember that praise and thanksgiving are paramount. They are the walls of the well into which flow all my blessings. As I give thanks, may my spiritual life be refreshed as a drink of cold water refreshes my body when I come in from work.

I was reading and pondering this passage this morning: "The poor in spirit inheriting the earth." What *does* that mean? Who are the poor in spirit? What characteristics set them apart? What is meant by the earth and inheriting it? The poor, because they are so many, might take over the earth, but being poor in spirit is surely not equivalent to being hungry-poor. It's all somewhat of a puzzle and like Scarlet O'Hara, I'll put off thinking about it 'til another day.

Thank You for your presence and guidance with me as I spoke at the church. The observations of the research project were mine, but the ideas of the kingdom of God were Yours. The writer of Psalm 26 seems so brash in asking that he be tested in heart and mind. I have a hard enough time meeting the tests of daily life without having to pray for a few extras. God, life here is so pleasant, reading, walking, sleeping, playing Canasta, doing only the things that require no effort. Because the world is full of needs, it seems sinful to live a life like this. But I like it. I can understand how the rich can ignore the poor when I have these Crystal experiences. Let me not "retreat" too far.

Mae

★ ★ ★

Dear God,

The Graham book's thought for today begins, "I awoke heavy."* This morning I, too, "awoke heavy." After tea and toast and a hymn, I feel better, but my inclination is just to sit. That I cannot do. All of this seems so far from contemplation and prayer. Please take me with *all* of my faults, frailties and fears, and make of me something useful.

Yesterday was such a perfect summer day. We watched Jeff vault at the Conference Track Meet. I felt the anxiety as he went higher and higher and the exultation when he cleared the bar at 16 feet, 8 inches, hit the mat standing, turned and waved toward us. It was great. Then, after dinner, he presented me with his championship plaque. What a gracious, emotional, beautiful, thing for him to do! Even now, the emotion so overwhelms me that the words do not come out right. The day ended with a talk around the dining room table about my future. I ought to make the decisions definite and get on with it. I'm going to be 81 next year, and I just plain don't believe it. There must be some mistake. How did the calendar get so whopper-jawed!!!

I just thought of Dad's prescription for rearing children:

1. Give them a happy childhood for they live it twice; once in actuality and once in memory.

2. Give them a good education, for with it they earn a living and enjoy the good things of life.

3. Give them knowledge of right and wrong to the extent that one person can give that knowledge to another.

4. Finally, leave them no money with which to damn themselves.

I've done my best on the first three and no need to worry about the fourth.

Now I remember before You, for Your blessing, each member of my extended family . . .

God of love and truth and goodness, lead *me* today in the way of love, truth and goodness, Suddenly, I am so grateful, that like a child in school writing the same sentence over and over on the blackboard, I could fill the pages with I THANK YOU, I THANK YOU, I THANK YOU . . .

Mae

---

*Graham, *ibid.,* p. 30.

Dear God,
    Here I am
        seated in my comfortable chair.
    My mind filled with activities,
        today's work, the events ahead.

    I bring it all here,
        my thousand flitting thoughts
        that will not give up and lie still.

    Here it all is, Lord
        here to make some sense out of it
        here waiting for You to take over.

    I am here, Lord,
        You, too, be here.

I must be getting ready for the hour of prayer at Downey. I have been reading Buttrick's book *Prayer.** Years ago, I read it and when I came across it at a book sale, I felt I was meeting an old friend. Nothing I have read since is any better. Today, one sentence fits my mood. "Peace of mind depends on the body, the weather, on the grace of friends. We cannot leap out of our skins to live in some philosophic stratosphere." Amen.

Last night, in the reading group, we discussed the church's role in the problems of the world. I said I didn't feel the church was equipped to come up with the answers, but rather must keep asking if the suggested solutions were ethical and what basis of morality each had. The church might then offer support to the solutions which appeared to be the best, but should never take the position that one, and *only* one was right. Too many times, history has shown us the flaws in that. I would like to hear Your comments, God.

It is not so much doubting, God, as it is wondering, how much, as portrayed in the Old and New Testaments, is the result of men's (and a few women) thinking, hoping and dreaming. How is it possible for them to be so sure? Have they adequately and realistically understood who You are? Why is their judgment to be trusted more than ours? To whom do You speak?

Also, I am trying to know how to make Jesus more central in my life, trying to realize that He *is* Savior, wondering how much I

---

*George A. Buttrick, *Prayer.* Abingdon Press, 1942.

dare question. Do I dare hear the answer? God, I think we had better talk about this (me?).

I bring to a close another of these little books. They have helped me to focus on Your presence, to clarify my thoughts, to straighten out the tasks of the day, to remember others. And they have brought me strength and energy.

Thank You

Mae

* * *

Dear God,

My spirit sings this morning that You know me. I invite You to fellowship and conversation.

How deeply and thoroughly do I enjoy a fall day. There is a oneness with nature, a wholeness of being, hope for today and tomorrow. I'll stop with tomorrow, satisfied with the goodness of the present. Not often enough do I cut living down to the proper space of "take no thought for tomorrow, sufficient unto the day is the goodness thereof." [sic] I've spent two hours out trimming the hedges and then an hour of quiet and devotion. There are days when not much seems to happen during that time, but there are more days when I have been energized, my moodiness turned to cheerfulness and anxiety to praise. Such days have a different hue. Thank You.

I have been feeling so good this week, little physical pain and much peace of mind. The weather has been cool and the gardening pleasant. Hour after hour of pulling weeds. How could that be pleasant? As I pull, I think, "This will make it easier next spring for the flowers to grow." I want to plant at least one more spring.

I am thanking You for my blessings, but pondering why the body is so much in the forefront. I read about meditation and Zen, and want to make the "spiritual" values predominant, to rise above the pains of the flesh. I really believe, too, that the mind is so powerful it can control, but that is *not* true of *my* mind. God, show me the way. Sharpen my senses. May I see anew . . .

May I keep listening . . .
    Keeping my eye and ear open
    To the least whispers
    Of Your will as to
    What I should do.

Let me keep listening . . .
To the messages from the World,
To the muted whispers of the poor,
To the anxious glances of the heavy-hearted.

Let me keep listening . . .
To Your voice within me
To Your spirit which strengthens my will to do Your will.

Let me keep listening . . .
To the clues which urge me on the way
To the acts of kindness which tell me I am loved
To the hearts of people which say they need love.

God, keep me listening.

Mae

* * *

Dear God,

I wish You could really talk to me, God, and I wouldn't have to just speculate about Your guidance in my life—and right now, in particular, Your guidance of my body. There is the awful pain and I pray for release. I know faith has a great deal to do with answered prayer, but I am so uncertain as to how much faith I have and I have no idea how to develop it. Sometimes I talk as if I had it, and sometimes, I think I haven't enough.

I would see Jesus, too. I would know His presence. All the hymns this morning have dealt with knowing Him and I still don't feel that I do. Is it sin that I cannot feel He died for me in any personal way? So many feel a personal touch of Christ (or say they do). I have felt only the Holy Spirit. Until now, I have felt that was enough. But now, God, I would like to know Jesus. Would it help to pray to Him? But He Himself said, "Pray to your Father, who is in Heaven." Patience, please, with my theological myopia.

My study of the scriptures always stimulates. What did You mean, "Have dominion"? Is it power over all living creatures? Does the Bible give justification for it? There is no way for us to control insects except by extermination, but dominion means that, too. Is this the first basis for violence? Is it this dominion that humankind wants to extend to all people? Is struggle for power built into the human race?

71

Children play because there is nothing else to do. Adults play for escape, but also for sheer enjoyment. If play is enjoyment, then some people find play is work. How many of our colleagues, as they come to retirement, say, "I loved every day of my work"? I did!! (And I still do!)

Last year, I wanted the maple saved. It died. Now I have a new one. I want to help it grow, so I must water it. I want to grow, too. Water my soul, God, from the wellspring of Your love.

★ ★ ★

Mae

Dear God,

The world is beautifully white this morning and I think of Crystal Lake. I like the white world, but I have a love affair with Crystal.

Ruth Bell Graham writes, "I pray—but nothing comes out right. My thoughts go flying everywhere."* God, I cannot keep my mind in neutral or on a plateau when I am praising and worshiping You. My thoughts go flying everywhere. It is as though a thought started down a path in my mind, but along the paths are hundreds more leading away from it. At each entrance there is a magnet which draws me into that path. I have gone no way at all, when I see more paths leading off from the original and automatically step into those paths. Some of the teachers of meditation say, "Do not resist that. It may be God's way of calling. Follow it." But, if I do that, I am like a water spider darting first in one direction and then off in another. It appears to be crazy with activity and never reaches its destination. I need to focus, for the retreat stands out in front of me in stark reality and I'm beginning to feel the thoughts coming. Help me with the sorting and organizing and help me not to be smug, or feel I have a higher truth, or more enlightenment than others. As You know all too well, I do not.

The semi-blackout last night was frightening. I thought, "Maybe this is death." Help me to handle whatever situation comes. The strange tingling in my heels and feet told me strange things were happening to my body. "It" passed, and I wondered, "What next, when again?" Do help prepare me for what is in store. I am so dependent on freedom from pain in order to be a "good" person that it is frightening.

Be with the reading group tonight. May our conversation not be gossip. May we help each other with love and support.

*Graham, *ibid.*, p. 111.

Thank You for the day when I feel Your presence within, when You move beside me, when You surprise me with something delightful, some action or blessing I was not expecting, like the invitation to go to Jamaica. Thank You that at this age I am able to do so much. Thank You for Yourself, God.

★ ★ ★   Mae

Dear God.

It's a beautiful, sunshiny morning. It's cold and the sun glistens on the ice-covered windows. Thank You for the heat which just now came on. How marvelous is a thermostat that turns on the gas, that brings the heat, that makes me comfortable. How marvelous the minds that worked out such a system. How marvelous is Your gift of creativity. How marvelous that on this little planet, in the sea of infinite space, we can live and work, rejoice and sorrow and find life good!

Last year I wrote, "A person of God inhales peace and exhales blessings." Help me to remember that, but, God, I am scared. When the near blackout times come, I do not know what to do. If it is the forerunner of a stroke, please, please may it not happen on the highway. Help me to trust You. Help me to know what to do when such a feeling comes. This morning, there was another frightening experience of not being able to stand upright and walk. Fortunately, there were things to hold onto, but it would have been impossible to walk across a room. I would have pitched forward. You know all of this, God, but I do need You to guide my faltering footsteps and my mind.

I have the responsibility of working with the Chi Rho youth group. I get a panicky feeling. Can I get across to them? What do I have of worth to pass on? Can I have them meditate for a few minutes and have it worthwhile? Put seeds into my mind so I can cultivate them during these next two weeks. How serious is the age gap? What should I do about it? It has never seemed important to me, and for years, I paid no attention to it. I made friends with all. I do not want to join the Senior Citizens!

Last night, five of us sat in this small, cozy living room before the fire and read and talked. God. you know about friends, how they help and gladden my heart. I feel swamped right now with the names and faces of people for whom I ask Your guidance . . .

This day, let joy sweep out of my life and into the lives of others.

Mae

73

Dear God,

Alas, I have slept too long and now must go to church for the prayer group. I will have to come back to this writing, but gratefully, I do not leave You here, for You go with me.

....

I am ashamed at my inability to communicate with You today. The dry bones of Ezekiel are the dry bones of my own inner life—compassion, love, prayer, giving, searching, "keeping at it." God, these dry up at times and I lose interest and even strength to do those things which give quality to life. But all these are within me and Your spirit says to my spirit, "Speak to these bones. Tell them I will enter into them . . . they will be energized." I seem to be spiritually deaf today.

It's strange the emotions that intertwine within me about prayer. I can believe in it so firmly and yet in some particular circumstance, I wonder if it works. Lead me to understand. I feel that as I pray for others, something happens. (I'm not clear what). But I also wonder if the thing which is accomplished is only my satisfaction from trying to be helpful. Help me to understand. Speak louder, please!

I have just listened to a TV program where the preacher talked about the "infallible Book." But, God, those books were written by humans. Did You actually guide their fingers and their thoughts so that You, and only You, directed what they wrote? It seems that the Bible is filtered through individuals, and while they were motivated by thoughts of You, they still had their own personalities, with all the weakness that implies.

God, do You need our prayers to carry out Your plan? If You do, (and I believe You do), then I will continue to be a part of Your larger plan and bring before You these friends . . .

God, help me to be worthy of little Irene's prayers. She is so dear. It was an astonishing revelation and a great help to me. My face is so aged that I must look like a "sour puss," but I want the joy I feel to show through to her.

Brighten now my day, I pray.

★ ★ ★   Mae

Dear God,

Thank You for delicious sleep. I awoke so refreshed. I lay there surrounded by my blessings. I sat up and hugged them to me with thanksgiving. You who love me and live within me, I rejoice because of Your love. You are the reason for my daily happiness.

Help me to love what I ought to love, make me worthy to love, courageous to suffer and faithful to suffer. Love is sweet and daring. Let me love You more than myself and base all my other loves in You. Amen.

"In everything, give thanks," Paul says, and today, I do.

Gratitude for—
> A son who is near
> Friends who love me
> A mind that thinks
> A church that challenges

Thanksgiving I offer You for—
> The measures of health and wealth You have provided
> For a cozy house which is home
> For a doctor who cares
> For the sense of Your presence.

Thanks I bring You for—
> The fruits and vegetables which nourish my body
> For books which both disturb and delight
> For the out-of-doors, daily, magically, becoming more beautiful
> For the promise of the future.

Thank You, God.

Let me now "frame the day's activities with prayers," with worship, with study, with friendship, with labor.

> I enjoy trying to think of new ways to tell You about life!

I am having a hard time living with my conscience, since I don't want to go to "Bible study." If I go, I hate it. God, would You please take over, but if that means going anyway, then I don't want You to. Like a child, I want You to argue with me, so I can try to justify my actions. If this is a sin, and I expect it is, You cannot forgive me, for I am not repentant.

I look back over the years of my requests to You and I want to comment, God, on Your care and loving kindness. Some of the people I have had no contact with, but I want again to think of them with love and name their names for Your blessing . . .

Mae

Dear God,

Let me practice what I preached at New Palestine last night. Let me "out-love." Bless the pastors in their ministry. Bless the church as it serves. Be with us at Downey that we may serve wisely. Help me with the youth group. Guide me as I buy gifts for Christmas. Be with all of us who have a part in the Christmas chapels. As I write You, my mind races ahead to things I can and should do. Thank You for an alert mind and a body that functions. May I use these blessings well. Live in me today, pray for me, take my life and use it.

As people think of the retreat just past, may their lives have been enriched. May all good remain and the gloss be washed away. Some questions remain for me. Through the years, I have felt Paul gave women a dirty deal. He thought he was doing us a favor by comparing us to the church, but he was audacious in comparing a husband to Christ. Woman a "helper" may be, but that does not make the helper subordinate. In fact, God *helps* His people—*All* of them.

While I am on the subject, I have also been critical of the many times Paul talks of himself. This morning as I read Philippians, it seemed to me that he might be doing part of it because he wanted to *share* himself with his friends. We want to do this all the time. It comes out in my frequent "I want to tell you about . . . " Help me to know how to use this insight in the next retreat.

God, can't You give me some clearer direction as to what I should do about going to Foxwood? I hate to put the "savings," made possible in my home, into an apartment, just to live a few years in comfort. The over-arching concern of these days is what plans I should make for the future. I feel as if I am a huge rubber band, with "pullers" on each end. One pulling to Foxwood and the other to 238 Ohmer Avenue. Won't You please join one or the other of the "pullers"?

I would praise You with word and life. Your loving kindness has been beyond measure. Gracias.

★ ★ ★   Mae

Dear God,

All letters and cards have been sent (and over 200 received) and all packages delivered. Now piled by the fireplace, to be opened tomorrow afternoon, are my gifts. Friends will bring theirs, and before the cheery fire, we will enjoy each other's presents. We will have high tea, then gifts, and then to church for the 7:00 services.

"Joy to the World"
The sun shines this December day
It shines in my living room
It holds warmth and cheer
It draws me into a circle of joy.

It heightens the delight of the Christmas season
It is like a magic wand
Moving ever so slowly across the room
Bringing to life all that it touches.

So is the coming of the Christ child
Moving across the days of our lives.

As I go through the building, wishing the staff a merry Christmas, may the greeting show in some unmistakable way, that I am able to do it only because of You.

Last night, Margie said, "I feel so comfortable having God around. I've never hear His voice, but He touches my shoulder." We were discussing prayer and the hurricane. Some said the people in Corpus Christi were convinced God had answered their prayers. I don't know, maybe there was more faith in Corpus Christi, the kind that moves mountains. I wonder if this is a good analogy? Someone asks why is there electric light in one house and not in the one next door. The answer is so simple. The folks in the dark house did not make the connection by paying their bills. We understand so little about how spiritual laws operate. How can we know if You lessened the hurricane as an answer to prayer?

God, You notice how I slur my words now. If it is some deterioration of the brain, will You please take away my human life and give me eternal life before I become too bad? There are so many indications my mind is going. All of this fills me with a sort of terror. When I work outside, I can ignore it, but in the house I am in a state of anxiety.

Be my timekeeper today that our hours will not be wasted or used amiss.

Mae

★ ★ ★

Dear God,

This morning I'm homesick. How, pray tell, could one be homesick living in a home in which she has lived for 40 years and been happy? The family will be all together in East Lansing and I won't be there. I remember so well the thrill I had when the family went to the Christmas Eve service when I was sick in bed. They came back and, standing in the hall, sang all the carols and hymns which had been sung in the service. It was lovely!

From my "early years," there stands out our first tree. Mom and Dad had decorated it after we went to bed. As I came down the steps in the morning, I stopped in astonishment, and held my breath, as I saw the candle-lit tree. The surprise and beauty were unlike anything I have since experienced. Another Christmas produced a small round fur muff. After writing this, I feel more homesick. Why is it Dree I want to see so badly? But I am not alone. People by the millions have been opening gifts this morning. May the joy become a residue of love and the disappointment evaporate.

This bitterly cold day is bright with sunshine. The house smells good with baking pecan pies. I am comfortable. I talked happily with the family last night. May they have a "joy day."

Thank You for all the people who remembered me with Christmas greetings, most of all, the one from Jeff saying he loved "showing me off to his friends." May I remember love and laughter toward others this day with prayers and praise for You, God.

Mae

✳

7

1981

Q. Is it all right to ask You for anything I want?
A. Not when I begin where I want to come out!

Dear God,
I cannot find my current book, so I use this page to say, "Good morning, I wish You well today in Your work, and relating to Your world." Relationships require the action of two parties, and You can be depended on to do Your part, but we respond so casually. Help me to know the true value of unconditional response.

What do You require of me? An evening of helping others? Oh, God, do be with me, that the study group will go on their pilgrimage with joy, through the dark woods of doubt, the sunlight plains of praise, the quiet evening of reflection, beside the dancing waves of expectation (and with *no* regrets for missed TV programs).

Help me to keep "walking." There is such a temptation to just quit and say "NO" to everything I am asked to do. Give me strength to walk and to walk straight, physically and spiritually.

This is silly to mention, but it's interesting, God, that it took a man to come along and drive the car out of the snowy driveway. I feel safer in a storm to have a man at the wheel, and yet I insist that women can do things as well as men. There is some flaw in my thinking. Perhaps it is the experience of a person and *not* their sex that counts!

Let me think my thoughts before You, and let me think Your thoughts after You. Let me live *before* You, in Your presence, so that others will live more happily and I more worthily. Grant, Oh God, strength and courage to dear friends. May their suffering be minimal. As we hear of new cases of cancer, we all shudder for the one who has it, and then we cry out, "Who is next? Who is next?"

Help me to keep in touch and in tune with You. "Thou art mighty and strong to help," and I pray for that help:
In relationships with family and friends
In ability to carry my responsibilities
In an attitude of love and helpfulness
In wisdom as to what I should do
In skill to let Your love shine through
In contacts with youth
In health, that I may function well.

Be present, I pray.
The sun shines brightly on this first day. Have a good year.

Mae

* * *

Dear God,
The sun shines brightly on this cold winter day, but it cannot penetrate the frozen earth. So is Your love, shining down on hard minds and spirits of those determined to hold power even by force. But there are some places where the sun is effective. So it must be with Your love. Let Your Son creep into the crevices of our hearts and minds. Let Him come into me, too, so that my heart may be thawed.

How grateful I am for this time of quiet to start the day. Thank You for this place, this chair, this lamp, this pencil and notebook, for all the so-called common things that are priceless for daily living.

I have sent off my money for Foxwood! Guide me as to when I should enter. There is some of the peace which passeth understanding these days. It is wonderful. The anxiety about the future is gone. Thank You for helping me make the choice to go. Continue, Oh God, to give me the opportunity to work these next two years and make adequate preparation mentally and physically. With Dag Hammarskjold, I say, "For all of the past, "thanks." For what shall be, "Yes."

My prayer life deepens, but it also deepens my frustrations over my failures. I read of the saints and their devotions and what I do is so simplistic, so devoid of depth, so far from the awe I am supposed to have, that I wonder if I should keep this up. The journals the saints kept are full of their smallness and Your greatness, so conscious of their sins, so filled with petitions for forgiveness, so overcome with their sense of Your ministry. And I go right along thinking of You as the greater and more loving personality of Dad. He loved me, I felt it in my bones. You love me, I feel it in my bones, regardless of my inability to portray You in the manner of the saints. Guide me in my understanding of You. I feel as if I can talk to You about You, and that You get the drift of what I am trying to say. I feel myself to be a mouse quivering in a corner hole, looking out at a great cat, ready to devour me. The cat is the future. I do not want to face it. There is nobody who understands me. All of the cheery words, "You are not that old" or "Come on. Everything is going to be OK" don't help. I guess I want understanding, not sympathy. But, God, I do feel You understand, that You say, "Sure, you can feel that way. It is tough. You can be frightened, even in despair. But remember, I am with you."

On this day I pray that the sunshine of Your presence may fall upon . . . As my life touches other lives, may their days be happier or more peaceful because our relationship is one of love.

Mae

★ ★ ★

Dear God,

I am so sleepy this morning, that I could not even sing songs of praise with enthusiasm. How sweet is sleep. How rewarding is a night when the mind seems to leave the body and in some quiet, silent place enjoys peace.

Here we are, well into the new year, and here I am, well into this day. Spiritual Companions come here tonight (and I promised vegetable soup, which means a trip to the store). The first hour and a half of each day is well established now, God. I am slow getting started so it takes more than an hour to get dressed and have breakfast (I used to do it in less than half that time). Then I settle myself in the Swedish chair for a period of quiet. I begin with some relaxing and settling-in exercises, devotional material in both Spanish and English, with the reading and pondering of a chapter of the Bible suggested by one of the readings. I then read the letters I wrote to You, from the year before, and write another for the day. This gives me the chance to pray again for any I prayed for last year. Before going to bed, I read back over several year's letters. This sensitizes me to former needs and requests. I conclude the period of "practicing the presence of God," by singing a hymn and a few minutes of quiet, putting the day into Your hands. In Your presence, I get up energized and, in various degrees, ready for the activities of the day.

But, my days still slip away, not at all like I want them to. I mean to get so much done in the yard at the Missions Building and I end up accomplishing so little. There are constant interruptions, though it is so hot, I wouldn't accomplish much, interruption or not. Yesterday afternoon, Mel and I went looking for trees and shrubs. I get tickled at how people think I know so much about gardening and plants. I'm always being asked questions. It goes to show that an evidence of interest and some hard work in any area tends to make one an expert! The same is true in the devotional life. I'm a learner (pilgrim is the technical term) in the strictest sense of the word, but because I am enthusiastic about prayer and have a relationship with You, and let that creep (bounce in at times) into my conversation, I am asked to speak on the subject. So I have accepted *three* requests to speak. See me through!

Mae

Dear God,

Here I am again, intentionally putting myself in Your presence, deliberately seeking Your help.

I have pneumonia and I fear high blood pressure. I was so frightened with the nosebleed yesterday. God, why do I get so scared, and all of this time I insist death holds no terror? Each time something like that happens, I think of Foxwood. It is beginning to sound like a haven to me, but I certainly hate to put all my money into just my care when my death would release the money for some good causes. What would You have me do with my time and my remaining strength, God?

We all live frightened these days, God. Afraid of illness (cancer) for those we love and ourselves, afraid of break-ins, of mugging in the streets, of intentional violence, of hatred. Tempers flare so easily. How, Oh God, do we bring Your spirit to bear upon society and have it present in our own lives? How do we hold on to hope or are we suffering the result of our own sins and suffering is the only way to salvation? I feel so helpless and hopeless about ways of improvement and yet I am not willing to give up. You are there. You are here. You are love. You require justice. I accept Your presence. You are within me. I take a deep breath, and try to think of words to describe You. I cannot. The best I can come up with is *Presence*. Some force, energy as invisible as the air I breathe, and yet as necessary for existence.

God, I feel as if I should be writing some contemplative thoughts instead of just listing my friends, but listing then seems more important . . .

Thank You for Your presence in my life!

Mae

★ ★ ★

Dear God,

I am so eager to get on with *The Other Side of Silence** that I would rather read than write you. Perhaps reading is another form of writing, just as singing is a form of prayer.

Am I growing in any way? It seems to me I am more open to ideas, more tolerant in my attitudes toward people, more understanding of others' needs, more sure of Your love, but less sure of my Christology. Guide me in understanding Jesus Christ and the place He has (or should have) in my life.

---

*by Morton T. Kelsey (Paulist Press, 1976)

I have been putting off getting into "cold print" my reactions to the session on prayer last night. It may prove to be more of a task than I want to attempt. I was disappointed in myself. As usual, I had too much to say and toward the end talked too fast instead of using pauses, so people could stay with me. I am grateful, God, that everybody seemed so interested. Now, it is my prayer that whatever there was of value will remain and whatever of triviality will be forgotten.

"The only way there can be unceasing prayer is to think *before* God, not *of* God." You already know that, so I am the one who must deliberately put my thoughts *before* You. Who am I that You should be mindful of me? I am Your child, Your daughter. As I embody some traits of my Dad, may I have within my being some of Your love and grace.

How does it work when I pray for somebody I never see anymore, nor have any contact with? Does my prayer act like a switch, and mentioning the names to You flips the switch so that light falls upon them? As many thoughts go flying before me like leaves before a gust of wind, I can pick up each thought like a dry, brown leaf and hand it to You. I pray now for each one of the Sunday School class, not dry, old leaves, but vibrantly alive youth.

Yume was here, with her parents, for dinner Monday and wrote in my guest book, "I am deeply happy to be your friend." What a lovely, gracious thing for anybody to say, and to have it from a 10-year-old is so gratifying! Do adults hesitate to get involved with youth? It appears they do, and they rationalize by saying youth is interested only in youth, so there's no point in trying a contact. True, it is risky and one can be repulsed, and even hurt, but I sense a longing on the part of youth to be recognized. If I can be of service, speak to me, God.

Willingly Yours,

Mae

★ ★ ★

Dear God,

There are some days when I have nothing to say. There are days when I am so troubled about assignments that I feel fretful. But almost always, if I breathe deeply and think of You, "Let Your grace descend upon me . . ." I can feel it descending, falling over my shoulders and enclosing my body. It is not heavy like the "armor of God." It is apt to give me wings with lightness. I can more lightly, gaily, joyously, gratefully, let Your grace descend upon me that I may live in peace and love all others—ah, that's the hard part, loving all others.

It is such a beautiful world.

The snow falls so quietly,
    turning everything into beauty,
It was such a wonderful night
    with seven hours of constant sleep,
        making this day a glorious beginning.

My body and mind function together
    so there is a unity of living,
        a sense of well-being,
A promise of things to come!

The devotional reading says that people are crying out, "Do you love me? Do you love me?" That was what she meant last night when she asked, "Do you really want to take me downtown?" I rudely answered, "I wouldn't have asked you if I didn't want to take you." If I had just said, "Sure, I want to take you," I would have answered the real question, "Do you love me?" God, the awful truth is I don't love very many people. For many I feel gratitude, admiration, respect, compassion, but I can count on the fingers of two hands those to whom I can say, "I really love you."

That You love me, I know, for You are faithful and trustworthy. But what does that really mean? That You are around me like the air, and that as the air breathed into my body helps me function, so You are there to keep my soul in peace, encouraging my spirit, assuring me that I need take no thought for the morrow. You see, God, I started out to focus on You and ended up with Me, the thing I do almost always. You are *Creator*, not just of the universe, but of my hand and of the pencil with which I write. You are lover of the world and of all that is in it. Since I am in it, *You love me.* You gave Jesus. Does the parent have the right to *give* his child? No, I think You sent Him. Do my simple, childish questions and doubts bother You, God? If they do, I'm sorry, but not apologetic. It's just that there is so much to learn and I don't have a great deal of time in which to do it!

Thank You for the Spiritual Companions and the painful growth which has come through that enriching discipline. Be with them and bless them. Help me to learn how to wait quietly before You.

Mae

★ ★ ★

Dear God,

"Be perfect as Your Heavenly Father is perfect." What does that mean? That just isn't possible. There must be some particular attitude Jesus is talking about and even so, how is it possible to reach perfection? The nearest I can come to it is *persistence.* I won't give up, and regardless of how I act or the world behaves, You keep right on trying and loving. But I can't even be perfect in that, for I get tired and quit trying, at least not trying up to my potential.

My inner spirit groans within me. Did a night of almost no sleep bring it on, or is it something much deeper? Was the rapping at the door which kept rousing me a little demon or my guardian angel trying to get in to help?

"O Lord, my heart is not lifted up. My eyes are not raised too high, but I have calmed and quieted my soul." This verse is my mood for today, except I haven't calmed and quieted my soul very well. Did the Psalmist do it all by himself? Or, was there a pause after the question, and *You* did it, but *he* took credit for it?

Right now, life seems so full of rather trivial matters and I stay in such a state of hurry. My mind races on to what I need to do, instead of concentrating on Your glory, greatness, power, love; the things we are admonished to do when we worship.

I walk and I am weary. I cannot walk straight. I cannot lift my feet. I shuffle. I weave to and fro. I feel uncertain all the time. I have distress that I feel so old with so little control over my body. My eyes hurt, they do not focus well. I have the same feelings that the Psalmist had at times. I am not vigorous. I am fearful. Why can I not move with some pep and energy? My mind is the same way. It feels drugged. I cannot remember. I constantly lose things.

86

Yesterday, I lost a prescription, a picture and a watch. All of this I find frightening. I gave some books to a friend and have no recollection of it. I said I would call her and completely forgot. God, can You help me or is this deterioration of the flesh?

It's strange, God, how much I think about going to Foxwood. It is as though having decided to go, I want to get it over with, but I look around at this home and I don't want to leave.

Well, I really have been "Negative Nellie" this morning. Forgive my lack of faith. Feeling sorry is harder than feeling jolly, so help me to take the easier path as I walk this day with You at my side.

Mae

★ ★ ★

Dear God,

A new book, a new week, a new day. Take it and make it Yours. You gave it to me.

As I start this book, Katherine has just started a new life. How suddenly this one ended for her. She was so concerned about selling her house and getting rid of things. Now, it makes no difference. Thank You for her life and all the good things she did, for her friendship, helpfulness, for the opening of her home on New Year's Eve (her constant hospitality) and for her dedication to the church.

All of this makes my own death more definite. What should I be doing to prepare for it? Help me to know if any loose ends or loose relationships should be tidied up. I should live with two points of view. This is my last active day, and how can I live the next decade wisely. Both of these viewpoints have to be kept in focus. Help me, God Almighty.

God, today I celebrate all Christian women.
All who have an eager desire to know and reach You.
I celebrate womanhood, sisterhood, my own femaleness
And Your Androgyny!

Oh what a beautiful October day.
Oh what a joy to feel well!

I will praise the Lord
For all His goodness.

I will sing to the Lord
A special song.

A song of Allelujah
With grace notes of Amens.

I will remember others
In my gladness.

I will call on Thee, Lord,
In their behalf.

I have seen love,
In the faces of my family.

I have known joy
In the presence of friends.

Peace has come upon me
In the company of God.

Faith has increased
In the time of prayer.

I have known the love of God!

Mae

★ ★ ★

Dear God,

Today is Maundy Thursday and it is a beautiful day. May we feel Your presence, Lord, know You are here blessing us, revitalizing, energizing us with strength, will and determination to make the world community better.

> May weakness of the body melt away,
> flabbiness of the mind disappear,
> inertia flee before the rays of the sun.
> May I rise from the chair renewed and may
> You be present in all my contacts with others.

But, Oh God, how easily the fabric of my faith gets torn. It is like the retina of my eye: thin, delicate, necessary for vision. Some time ago, I wrote, "I would place my hand on the book of fear and say I will not park here," and a year later, I have failed to live up to that high promise. I do fear I have lost the keys. I lost the Christmas ornament. A fork and two spoons are gone. I am constantly hunting things. I am afraid of the loss of power to work, to function. I got arrested for not stopping and going through on a yellow light. The fine is $40! What a dumb way to spend money when it is so scarce.

Such a strange dream I had last night. The family was going on a trip. We came to a body of water with stones piled irregularly to make a crossing. I said to Dad, "You can't cross that," but he drove on over the rocks that I was sure we could not cross, and got to the other side. After I scrambled up and followed, I thought, "I'm always trying to stay with Dad. This seat belongs to the one who helps." What is the relationship, for me, regarding "God" and "Father"?

Now the bright sun shines on the fireplace. It shines not only through the windows, but on the leaves of the trees, tossing wildly by a brisk breeze, making shadows move in the light. It is as though something alive were in the room. Can my life be like that? Your love shining through me, casting light in other places? May whatever light my life casts on those about me be as genuine and as real.

Mae

★ ★ ★

Dear God,

Last year I wrote a poem on being 80. What unnecessary anxiety I put myself through. Eighty has been one of the very best years of my life, in spite of pneumonia. I have rejoiced in countless things to do. I have felt freedom from severe pain. I have gloried in another Spring. The moments with You each morning have become more important to me. I want for others the satisfactions and the blessings which have come to me.

Now, thank You for the good physical, mental and spiritual feelings I have today.

Let my cry come near before You. Give me understanding, according to your word.

Let my pen write words of praise, for I am thankful.

Let my words be those of kindness and good counsel.

I have seen Your presence in the actions of my friends, for You have made a difference in our relationships.

Let me never be discouraged to the point of despair, for You are God, and have the power to change all things.

Let me realize constantly that you are present and will provide.

The church service yesterday was *good*. Filled with meaning, music, and spirit, all intertwined so as to both heal and challenge. I trust it is all right to be pleased with compliments from youth. The pleasure is that I am perceived by them not as a "stodgy old woman." Sue told me this morning at the table she was reading the names of the CWF officers and remarked, "They are all getting older." Kent spoke up, "All but Mae Ward. She is just 39." Beth said after the session, "You are a soft, sweet breeze blowing through my life." Such comments give me a great sense of self-worth and I'm grateful and humbled, God.

How afraid should I be of You? I know Jesus told us to be afraid that You would cast us into hell, but He told the story of the son returning home to be received by a loving father. Why should I be afraid of You any more than Don Jeff should be afraid of me? That You created the universe and also love *me* . . . and in the reality of these extremes, I stand in great awe and wonder.

Are You far away, high and beyond me? Yes, of course. Are You dwelling within me, ready to give guidance every minute? Yes, of course. How, then, should I worship Thee? "Be still and know that I am Your God." Of course!

Mae

★ ★ ★

Dear God,
  I am sorry when I do not begin the day with You. It is my loss
indeed . . . Right then my mind went trailing off thinking of the
dirty windows, and how to crowd in next week all that has to be
done. Be with me in the little nagging things of life. Let me use the
desires of the day as the will of tomorrow. Discouraged, but never
despairing!
  As I reread my letters with their requests to You, I feel as if I
am reading scripture. Is that too bold and daring an idea? But I
"make my requests known" and You answer. I try to relate to You
and there is evidence that You do direct. I go on "claiming"
Health, and in a perfectly marvelous way you grant it. I mowed
the lawn without exhaustion. I worked on research 'til midnight. I
claim only what You grant and teach me the connections that
make healing possible. *Power* to continue to "be present," to
understand, though the quick emotions still come upon me
before I can stop them. I claim power to know how to help
others, the family, the Sunday School youth, the sick. *Joy* that
comes almost always in the midst of death and talking with
friends and loved ones in grief. *Sufficiency,* this You provide, Oh
Lord, and in a marvelous way. Help me to trust You into the
future. (I have a fear that after I have talked so bravely, I will fail
at the "testing time.")
  I keep on praying, hoping that prayer helps, but half fearful
that it won't. I want to trust You completely, and that I do in the
long run, as Jesus did. But, He prayed to avoid the cross and You
saw fit to let Him have all the suffering. That is what I mean. I
pray for the painless path and You may not permit me to have it.
In that case, has my prayer had any value, any weight with You?
  Am I more of a Jew than a Christian? It is easy to understand
Romans 8:38-39 and its emphasis on Your love, but the
stumbling block is, that it is through Christ Jesus. Jesus showed
us how to understand, but hasn't Your love for us always been
present? When I say I am a Christian, what am I saying?

l. I accept Jesus as the person who most fully made You known to us.

2. I know no other way to declare my belief that You are God and God is love.

3. I try to accept and follow the teachings of Jesus as the basis for the best kind of life here on earth.

But, that He *died* for *me* is still too hard for me to understand.

I'm sorry!

Mae

★ ★ ★

Dear God,

I am a space shuttle moving about in the vastness of Your love and truth, hunting for more information on the laws which govern my behavior as I relate to You. Thank You, God, for what I already know of Your love.

I know, as You do, that I am losing my sight. Today, Dr. McCord verified it, though I was hoping against hope that it was my imagination. I cannot read a single line of print with my left eye. He offers no hope that the sight will improve. It's discouraging and disheartening, but I cannot believe I will go completely blind. Living may be much less pleasant, and may even become very difficult. I am sure I need to get to Foxwood.

I ask now for guidance about the selling of the house. Rough weather is coming and, if it be Thy will, shelter me from the storm.

I have a practical problem. Something new is called for at the communion table, God. Lead me in new ways, so that our fear of change, our sense of what we consider "dignity," does not make us leave out the joy and the "good news" in the celebration. Let me not fear disapproval if I dare to proclaim Your LOVE in new ways.

The prayer list grows. I have not spent much time thinking of each, just a few seconds. But, God, take the seconds and multiply the good which will result by seven-fold.

Let's keep in touch.

Mae

Sleep has flown off into a thousand bits, not to be collected despite hot milk at 2:00. I am obsessed with the fear of the loss of sight. Tonight I have looked in vain for the light at the end of the tunnel. It is not there. I have been a bird shut forever in a cage. I have beat against the wires. They did not give way. I flew to the other side and wildly beat against the wires. They held firm. Round and round I went, seeking some escape. Worn out physically and in despair emotionally, I sat on the low perch in the cage. Then a bit of hope came and I flew to the top perch. Even if I couldn't see, I could sing. But it was not singing I wanted. I wanted sight.

Please!

Mae

★ ★ ★

Dear God,

I sit down and write to You and sometimes, instead of doing that, I remember I have not taken my medicine, or unplugged the hedge clippers, or fixed my church envelope, and I wonder if I should jump up and do those things and then be quiet, or whether to make myself go on with "devotions," and then take care of the details. "Devotions" is a strange word for what I try to do. I *devote* the time, but what do I accomplish?

I would like to share with you the deep satisfaction which comes from my contact with young people. Before church, Cherrie stopped, put her arms around me and said nothing. Bill hugged me and said, "This makes it a good day." Kent came along to tell me of his paper route. Terry kissed me. Both Carla and Brenda threw their arms around me. After church, Beth came and hugged me. I said, "Beth, it's so good that you being young and I being old, can be such good friends." Beth said, "But you aren't old." "Yes, I am, Beth, in years, though I don't feel old." "See?" she said, "That's what I mean." I really feel I have had both a ministry and a great delight in bridging the generation gap.

Thank You that there is a place like Foxwood and I am permitted to go there. Thank You for the wonderful support of the family. As I prepare for the change in the next few months, guide and counsel me. I planned to do some sorting and packing every day, and have done none for a week. It seems terrible that I shall be putting all I have saved, all these years, into keeping myself in comfort instead of leaving it to others. Oh, God, help me to handle well what I possess, and even life itself.

Joy should characterize old age, because the years have brought experience and knowing what can be expected of life. Anxieties should be less, knowing that many worries never materialize and things work out. Yet, I forget *all* of the time, not just people's names, that's chronic, but now there is scarcely anything I don't forget. It's frightening. I forgot to mail a letter (and now I can't find it). Twice I have forgotten to get my umbrella at the building and have needed it. It's still there. I forgot to take my coat from the car . . . and now, as is to be expected, I have forgotten all of the things I intended to include in this letter! Writing this must be a form of punishment for my forgetfulness.

Until tomorrow, and its *new* start,

Mae

★ ★ ★

Dear God,

Here I am in the tranquillity and serenity of Crystal again. How blessed I am. The breeze is cool, the waves leap against the shore with their eternal rhythm. In the quietness of this place, it is hard to enter into the pain of the world.

I find vacationing with other people difficult. There are times of "chill," when one or the other is feeling left out, indifferent, or has just withdrawn for good reasons. Not always can there be warmth and sun. Clouds seem to float through or hover, as clouds block out the sun. Yet all of this is natural, but *I* want "sun" always in our lives. I want the impossible.

This is a marvelous place for study. As I read Psalm 119, I try to imagine what the person was like. The Psalmist is completely self-centered (and gives me some justification for these self-centered notes to You). He expects rewards for his good behavior. We are all in this boat. He brazenly points out how obedient he has been, and seems to brag about his knowledge of the Law and the Word. Only at the very end does there seem to be a bit of humility, but he closes with his old refrain of "I do not forget Thy commandments." My life and faith are too much like his, but I do not feel there are enemies out to devour me. I wonder what he did that resulted in the "wicked laying a snare" for him. There are some beautiful verses in the Psalms, but this has a ring of pure selfishness.   Psalm 78 is another problem. Are You really like the God of the Psalmist writes about? "The anger of God rose against them and He slew the strongest of them. He restrained His anger often and did not stir up all His wrath." Did You deliberately smite "all the first-born of Egypt"? Did You intentionally cause hundreds of babies to die of diphtheria in Buenos Aires in 1933? Surely, such ideas do not conform with the Father of the Prodigal or "God is Love." How much can we see You moving among us? Do You try to teach us something through the violence which exists, or is this the result of our sin? Do *You* provoke men to violence? God, at times I feel as if I know You well and am known by You, and again, I wonder if all my faith is just human longing for security. Help!

★ ★ ★

Mae

Dear God,

How beautiful is *Your* world, how beautiful is *our* world. How refreshing this breeze blowing across the blue of the lake. How satisfying it is to have friends. Three weeks have been a learning, growing experience. In spite of our differences, arguments, and moments of irritation, we will be closer because of this experience. But, in all honesty, it must be said, we each are happier living alone. Thank You for friends who love and support.

My praises to You this day are deep and genuine. Would I had the words to express them adequately! I keep trying, though my hymnology is rather rudimentary.

> Let me sing a song of praise
> Every hour of every day
> For the kindness of Your love
> Guides and sweetens all the way.

> Round about me like the air
> I am conscious of Your grace
> I will ever grateful be
> For the care You show for me.

My heart really overflows with joy because of the time I have had with Jenny and Don Jeff. The nights have been full of delicious sleep and the days with quietness. There has been good companionship, long hours of reading aloud and writing and some thinking. How do I express my thanks for such priceless blessings? May I be worthy of them. Last year I prayed, wondering if I had the right to pray for another summer like I had had. You granted me one even better. Thank You. Thank You.

. . . .

How easy it is to read scientific books and wonder, to the point of doubt, about You working in history. I have no trouble believing in You as Creator, for my mind rebels against thinking this world just happened. Logic, however, is against believing in You as a personal God, but logic has no power in convincing me in that direction. By whatever name You are known, You are a part of my life. You live in me. I am made in Your image and I know it. Why am I so sure of You? Because I feel Your presence and I sense a guidance in my life. As Dad still lives for me, though gone forty years, so You live because, at some time, in some place, in a specific way, our lives crossed, touched, then merged.

That is the miracle,

Here is my gratitude.

Mae

★ ★ ★

Dear God,

I am like a student starting college, eager for new experiences, frightened at the thought of all the newness. Wanting to go, not wanting to go. I am eager for the experience of the retreat and yet frightened. It was an awesome task to try to lead people into the spiritual life, especially when I know so *little*. I am so small. I have many needs. You have but one—that we accept Your love. I am trying, quite hard it seems to me, to come into a loving intimacy with You. It needs no effort on Your part. So, grant me some of Your ease of making contact. Give Your strength to me. Also show me how to love and give myself away. May some of the abandon that I would show running to a lover and throwing myself into his arms be true as I meet You today. Let Your grace be around me like a lover's arms. Let me feel the exultation that love provides!

To You I come
    Eager to know Your will
    Eager for your grace to fall upon me
God, to You I come
    Giving thanks for countless blessings
    Grateful for family and friends
    Conscious of Your greatness
    Aware of my weakness
    But acknowledging I also have strengths.
God, to You I come
    At the beginning of this day
    At the close of another week
    During hours of joy and grief.
God, to You I come
    Asking that Your love encompass
    Each and everyone I love.

Another wedding anniversary. How far away that day seems. Thank You for Your guidance through all of the years, though there were times when I was so overcome with my problems, I did not realize You were there. Memories, memories, memories: walking down the aisle in my rose-colored, net-over-grey-satin dress, astonished at how my knees shook. The dinner at the hotel, which seemed so plush, the many wedding gifts and the first night. September 25, 1926 was a day like today, beautiful, sunny and cool. The *best* days of the year are the Fall days.

I want to mention some people that I love. I am grateful for each. As I write their names, will You please be near to them?* These are the circles of friends among whom I live, who give me a sense of identity and meaning. How rich, how blessed, how wealthy I am. Thank You, my God.

Mae

✴ ✴ ✴

Dear God,

This morning I am an owl, staring into a bright light, blinking my eyes to see what is there. Help me now to focus on the light, which is Christ. May my eyes see Him clearly and my ears hear His words. But, Oh God, I do *not* see Him. I cannot imagine

---

*Seventy-seven individuals are given and their problems and needs noted.

myself physically in His presence. Such mystic experiences do not seem to be for me. My lot seems to be the practical, the down-to-earth, the simple offering of prayers for others. I cannot let it go. I would see Jesus, for the years lengthen and time grows short. You know, I pray to see His face and yet, I fear it. How do I handle this? I cannot bring myself to completely surrender.

Most mornings I look forward, eagerly, to the hour of reading and bringing my heart in tune with Your will. Today, I don't seem to care as much, but habits hold. I'm bothered by the experiences of Carl Jung, for I can't understand his experiences of receiving grace *after* his "sin," which, I guess, was his sin of doubting You. I am not sure. I want to think of You as a kind, loving Father. My own father carried to the Nth degree, not giving everything, but wanting for me everything which would make me a well, whole person, capable of living life to its fullest!

Most mornings, I read some portion of the Bible and often it is so familiar, I know it by heart and I wonder what is the point of reading it again. Yet, the "wise ones" say there is always something new to be learned. I do not necessarily find it so.

★ ★ ★

Most mornings, I look forward to reading the letters of past years, for they:

Give a sense of continuity to life
Show how many people need special help
Indicate how my (and others') requests have been answered
Remind me of past blessings
Prove that life is good with varied activities
Show a delight I have in this contact with You

Most mornings I think are wonderful in Your presence. If today is an exception, bear with me 'til tomorrow.

Mae

★ ★ ★

Dear God,

The time for this morning period of quiet was easy at the lake, but here the world is too much with me; hurrying I lay waste my powers. It seems so difficult to live serenely. I hadn't been in the house an hour when the minister was here, almost begging that I take the High School class again. I *almost* agreed.

It is true, I find this a precious part of the day, that I do look forward to it, that ideas, anxieties and fears get straightened out as I write You. Now, God, I earnestly ask Your guidance for the retreat, that I am able to adequately portray what meditation means and not give the impression I know it all, for God, You know how imperfect I am in this relationship, how I have failed.

Now, most of the trees show the design of their forms. Those which are not bare, soon will be, for the rain and wind bring the leaves down in a rush to reach the earth. The front yard is a solid carpet of damp, golden leaves. I think how quietly they lie there, and try to let some of that tranquility seep into my soul and quiet my spirit. How can I stay alert to "the wonders under my feet" and all around me? I would sense Your presence, feel the wonder of beauties around me, the marvelous workings of my own body, the possibility of knowing You are within me, the faith that the world (humanity) can come to know You. Thank You for the clues, the hints that come day by day, that this is Your world, that we *can* discover how to live in it with joy! Thank You for the loveliness I see in people, and for the discipline and steadfastness of my friends. I am indeed blessed.

Truly Yours,

Mae

Dear God,

It's a beautiful, sunny afternoon with the sun on the snow making the world glisten with glitter, a time to feast on beauty. That I do, with a fearful dread in my heart that my days of seeing are very limited. At church today, it was evident that my eyes are going. The side vision has been poor since the operations, but now, if someone comes up on the left side, he/she is a blur. I felt desperate. Even as I greeted them, I cried out, "God, Oh God, not so fast. Allow me a little more time to get used to it." The right eye is losing vision, too. How do I accept this? Can I accept it and not fall apart? I, frankly, *do not know.* Today I panicked. One after another, the operations have come and been endured. But can blindness be endured? Yes, if it comes, it has to, but with how much grace could I accept it, Lord? How will I be able to read Don Jeff's letters? How can I read the Bible or write You if I cannot see? Am I to learn that in darkness You are nearer than in light? Where are my inner resources now? Now I am seeing what I do not have. I have been quite courageous in life so far. Help me not to fall apart now. I've got to keep blessings before my eyes, not blindness!

Patience, Mae: There is no reason why you should not, *right now*, make an attempt to get inside a circle of quiet and absorb calmness. Travel with me, God, this day, I pray.

Mae

★ ★ ★

Last night I was reading *The Summer of the Great-Grandmother,** and burst into tears. I threw myself on the bed and sobbed. How unlike me. I felt sorrow for all the grandparents whose lives end in senility, complaining, ugly and incontinent. It all seems too unfair; to be strong, vital and alert and have it all end so dismally. It's not that I mind too much having that fate, but I don't want to be *remembered* as an ugly old woman, whining and helpless. I *don't* want to be remembered that way. I said it over and over, or really, I sobbed it over and over. No matter how beautiful and gracious life has been, we do remember those last days, weeks and months. Let that cup pass from me, I earnestly pray.

Maybe I am on the wrong track. I have wanted You, the all-powerful God, to intervene, to reward the righteous with health and prosperity. At times, You seem to do that, but more often than not, the good suffer. I need to keep in mind that You provide the power to *endure*. I bow my head to reverently say, "Thank You." I lift my head to take in all the wonders about me and say, "Thank You." The richness and beauty of Your nature are revisited in the bright colors of the leaves It is such a *good* time of year to be alive. "THANK YOU!"

Mae

---

*by Madeleine L'Engle (Seabury, 1980)

Dear God,

The ground is white, the sky is grey. It is Thanksgiving Day. I give You thanks for countless blessings along life's way.

I am so glad I have established a pattern of writing and praying. The fifteen minutes have grown into forty-five or more. Seldom do I make a request for a specific thing or request for others, but rather for a sense of Your presence and guidance for them. For myself, I pray for specifics, and, God, You can answer as You see fit. But there do seem to be astonishing answers to "little prayers" in my every day activities. Prayer is a joy and a delight!

I Cor. 2:10, "But God has, through the Spirit, let us share His secret: insight into the meaning of everything." Incredible! God, let us share Your secret. The secret of knowing why I am here!! The mystery of creation. The purpose of life. These are secrets, God, and they are baffling but . . . The "why I am here" can become enjoying God and the Creation. The "purpose of life," to praise God and love my neighbors. All of this doesn't seem reason enough for the outpouring of love and care others have bestowed on me. Or, on the other hand, for the heartache and sorrow that have been present during the years. I can only speak for myself, but it seems to me the best answer to the secret is—

God wanted me here. Since He wanted me here, He is with me. If He is with me, He provides the wherewithal to make my life count. His grace descends upon me to help me face the day. His love includes me, that together we add to the world's store of love and reduce its hatred.

I think this is true!

Choices! Decisions! Yes or No! My mind is like a whirly-gig perched on a stick. The wind sends it whirling in one direction and then in the opposite. Do I or don't I accept the writing assignment on prayer? It looms bigger and bigger. In the past, I have planted a lot of seeds and You brought forth the harvest. I believe You will do that again. Forgive me for a nagging doubt that for some reason that process might fail, as lack of water causes the seed not to sprout, my spiritual drought may make barren my effort.

★ ★ ★

Dear God,

I am a bunch of cut-up vegetables, lying on the counter, ready to make a soup. May I be all that is needed to make it good this day.

My mind fairly dances this morning as it dashes from one activity to another, always trying to be sure I don't forget anybody I should remember at this time of year, thinking of the program for which I have some responsibility. You see, God, how my mind seems to be working on each floor of a ten-story building. May the elevator work well as I cover all floors. At times it is overpowering, but it is wonderful to be able to "rise to the occasion."

Christmas activities fill the days and evenings My feeling of distaste about gift-buying, etc. has gone and I feel joyful and thankful about it all. May the spirit of peace prevail. Now I need to do the laundry, the shopping, and mail the small packages to Michigan. Why do I never feel satisfied with what I do for Christmas? Because the rest of the family is creative and their packages so attractive. No matter how I try, I *never* come up with any ideas, so I continue to give "practical gifts." I can't even wrap anything so that somebody might say, "Oh, what a pretty package." I have such high expectations for Christmas and hopes for adding Christmas cheer, but I'm no howling success at it.

But I am so happy and grateful for You!

God, You continue to create.
　　You create in me,
　　You create through me,
　　To make the Kingdom.
You use my prayers as a tool,
　　A technology to bring about changes.
　　First in myself,
　　Then in my environment.
Every small act of mine
　　Is important in the creation of myself,
　　and ultimately in the community in which I share.
　　Creator God, use me in Your acts of creation.

At times I say to myself, "Who are you, Mae, to think God is with you—the Almighty God and the little you?" But I do know You are, God!

Mae

✳

8

1982

"I watch the snowflakes fall, there is a fascination about them. They are so large, they fall so steadily. What do they tell me of my relationship to You? Gravity pulls them to the earth, but they assert their independence by whirling a few times before they land."

Dear God,

The sun shines, lighting and brightening the living room. There will be less sun shining at Foxwood, I fear, just one large window in each room. How I will miss the sun moving from object to object and making the room come alive. I must savor each moment of the sunshine time in my home between now and then. It was only a year ago I was praying for help in making decisions about the future. You answered that prayer and as I think back over the year, I believe You have led me in a very natural way (nothing special or spectacular), to this moment where all seems to be working out for my going to Foxwood. Thank You for daily guidance.

I have been reading *Creative Dislocations,* a very helpful book dealing with the major changes which happen in life. I thought he was writing to me about Foxwood, "to everything there is a season." But sometimes it's hard. Brown said, "For all of us, future dislocations loom, whether their content is job insecurity, spiritual spentness, the fear of death, the loss of family surroundings and dear friends, or the sheer tedium of a humdrum life. And I affirm, in the face of all that, that the dislocations can be given a creative content, not just because we determinedly will it so, but because we are sustained by grace, whether we call it that or not. So, hail to the dislocations. May they be grace-filled. Blessed be their name."* (It might not hurt to cross my fingers and knock on wood, too.)

During my working years, it was hard, but I practiced more or less faithfully, "Take no thought for the morrow. Your Heavenly Father knows your need." Now that a long, serious illness may affect me, I depend more on my savings (and they will not be enough) than I do on You, God. Help me to change and get things in perspective.

At the rate my eyesight is going, I may not be able to read this next year. Like Paul, I say, "See with what large letters I write You." God, may I not go blind. Keep the blood flowing into my eyes. Thank You for what sight I have and that I can still read. Oh, God, please grant my petition and let me continue to see!

Be with me as I plant today. Thanks for seeds and a place to plant them. Let's go get our hands into Your warm earth.

Mae

★ ★ ★

---

*Robert McAfee Brown, *Creative Dislocations* Abingdon Press, 1980, p. 144.

Dear God,

I thought I had carelessly left this book at home and then found it on the back seat of the car this morning. What a joy to find it. I have missed writing a note to You. Sure, I told You about life, but it was not the same. Writing satisfies something within. There is a longing to be understood. Writing provides an action and action produces results; it changes circumstances. Writing makes me face reality, though the reality may rightfully contain some wishful thinking. Putting the thoughts on paper somehow guarantees a response from You. I am keeping my part of the covenant, "in every way acknowledging You and waiting on You," so that Your response is to help me "walk and not faint." Are there angels who minister to us as they did to Jesus after the temptations? Is there a "guardian angel" for me? For each person? Does the "ministering" depend on our acceptance of it?

Again I dreamed of a house which leaked and my feeling that Dad ought to do womething about it. I have had that dream many times, though with varying details. What does it tell me about myself? I already know that I have "leaks," flaws in my character.

The sign "FOR SALE" will go up Tuesday or Wednesday and then I must be ready for people to come any day. I hope there are some.

I'm in a nostalgic mood. Dee had left here a large box which I opened in my sorting. It was filled with hundreds of Christmas cards. I have read messages of love and cheer to Dee and Allan, with words from people no longer here. People who laughed and cried, hiked and cooked meals, sent and received Christmas cards. I have no doubt that all who have left this earth are better off, and yet, this earth is good and they can no longer enjoy its goodness and beauty and rejoice with family and friends.

It has been a bitter-sweet evening. I feel keenly her absence. At the same time, I feel her closeness, for we were sisters in a very real way. So, the tears well up, though I would not wish her back. Her last years were dreadful. She prayed earnestly to die for months before her prayers, and mine, were granted. For her life I now give thanks. Help me to be an amplifier of hope and a bearer of good tidings.

Mae

Dear God,

After my last letter, I came across Eccl. 5:20. "God keeps man (woman) occupied with joy in his (her) heart." As I sorted stuff in the basement, I came across a poem I had fastened on the inside of my office door on June 23, 1941.

> "And if I cannot see the gleam
>   Shall I proclaim there is no light
> Because mine is a shattered dream
>   Shall others falter in fright?
>
> No, though my night be thick and black
>   Tho' I be sinking in despair
> For those who follow, I'll call back
>   Hope on, I know the stars are there."

I had been divorced. Norm had left ten days before Christmas and getting through Christmas is something I would rather forget. I had left Don Jeff in school in Cleveland, when I began work on April 15, 1941. The last morning I walked with him to school, explaining that he would come to me as soon as school was out and I found a house.

There was so much about my new job that I couldn't handle. Dr. Hopkins insisted I go to Mexico and I had returned feeling that I had made a mess of my first contacts with the staff, that they felt I was not capable of the job. I had plenty of doubts about myself. Do You remember, God? The despair, the inadequacies, The fear of how I could manage the home and be away so much, have now been blended with success, with trust, with love, but when I put the poem on the door, I was fighting hard and had to search for the stars. Now, this poem has, almost providentially, fallen into my hands and I feel that if I could come through the year '41 with expectations and joy, I ought (after all of these years of experience) to do it again in '81. God, if You are occupied with putting joy into my heart, I should be saying, "Hope on! I know the stars are there."

Guide me in every little detail of living. May I truly be clay in Your hands. Mold me anew.

Mae

★ ★ ★

Dear God,

Thank You for the rain and coolness. Thank You that twice yesterday, when talking with friends, I was able to think of You and ask Your help. I think I am learning, Lord. Have patience and stay with me. Though I may never have a great mystical experience, I pray for a daily feeling of Your presence.

> You live in me.
> Help me to recognize You.
> I live in You.
> Your grace is sufficient.

> How do I avail myself of Your grace?
> What wisdom is needed
> To know the method of using Your power?
> Is mere asking sufficient?

Jesus said, "Ask."
Jesus said, "Faith the size of a mustard seed wrought miracles."
I have that much faith.

> I'll ask!

A young couple looked at the house and have made an offer. I've been afraid it might be months before it sold and now I'm afraid they will want it as soon as possible. Tonight I'm jittery, because there are three months before I can get into Foxwood and I don't want to get out of 238 Ohmer too soon. Oh, life, life, what difficult choices you present!

What I will finally be getting from the sale of the house is going to be far below the asking price, but at this stage, I just want to get it sold and be on my way. It's strange. I never thought I would want to part with the pink house, but slowly and surely, I have been led to this acceptance. It has been a wonderful home through these forty years. I believe it *has* been a place where many people have felt comfortable and have enjoyed sharing joy and experiences with others. It has been *good* to live here!!

Thank You.

Mae

Dear God,

Today I feel free and buoyant. It is difficult to discover a pain. I feel as if I could "walk and not be weary." Have I suddenly realized You are keeping me occupied with joy? In spite of a malfunctioning eye, You know my name and the number of hairs of my head, so surely, You care about precious eyes, my eyes, once so brown and bright. Still, I have used them hard for many years. Let the blood flow with special favor, nourishing and healing.

I've been reading Paul, on the second coming of Christ. Is it really going to be that way? Jesus, with a great shout, coming into sight and people flying up in the air? I can't believe it. I believe that the method, the way of meeting Jesus is the same as the way I meet You each moment, communion of spirit with spirit. I can't see that it is important to believe anything about the second coming. If it is, You had better enlighten me, God!

Certainly it seems from my study that most of the Psalmists belonged to a "me generation." which must be why they have such an appeal for us. They are full of "my needs," "my desires," even "my enemies." This is a busy week and I, too, am full of "me-ness." May I take an hour at a time and manage it, eliminating the hurry that overwhelms me when I think of the week. Be in our midst, Oh God.

The Sunday service I am to lead looms big. Thinking of the seriousness of prayer, as Jesus agonized with drops of blood, and yet the happiness with which I come to these moments, gives me pause. What should I be doing to make them more serious, or is that necessary? Is what I do superficial? Is "warm-up" or "count-down" for prayer important? The "prayer amid pots and pans." Brother Lawrence would not have found it necessary, for he lived in prayer. A few times each day, I am able to do that, but mostly, "preparation" is helpful. Certainly, for me, prayer has a twinge of mystery and uncertainty about it, yet it is so basic to the Christian life.

> Prayer is praise, Prayer is supplication,
> Prayer is confession, Prayer is intercession,
> Prayer is thanksgiving, Prayer is silence
>
> Prayer is life!!

My mind has wandered upstairs, downstairs, searching for things to put into the garage sale and what price to put on them. I have debated about costs of moving and hoped and prayed that the right decision has been made. I have wondered how I can live in the home and yet move out. Moving is a stressful time! I wonder, are there any garage sales in Heaven, God, or is everything of great worth?

Mae

★ ★ ★

Dear God,

It's 2 a. m. and we have been having a very bad storm. So bad, one can't sleep. The house groans and creaks, as if it would fall apart. Allan and Helene came Thursday and have worked like dogs with the garage sale, and garage it was, for we had rain after getting everything set up in the yard. It was some garage sale, don't You think? How people bought! The Missions Building people came over, en mass, at noon. I could have sold all the furniture in the house twice over. It was sort of fun having a sale and watching people look over things, but frightfully tiring.

I have let the details of moving drop down on me "ker- plunk." There is so much to do and so little time to do it. I seem unable to organize my time. Help me get on with the sorting of years of papers, letters and mementos. May I act kindly when folks try to sweeten my departure. I honestly do not want farewell parties or moments of recognition. I must admit the entire moving experience has become oppressive and at times depressing. The time has finally come when my greatest desire is to get it over. Is it natural to feel this way, God? Good night again. I hope.

. . . .

This afternoon I have been going through drawers and throwing away things. How hard it is to throw away a beautiful card with expressions of love, but I did it. With a twinge of sadness, I permitted destruction to come to cards from friends. Bits of beauty that deserve to be preserved, but for what purpose? Letters from Babs, Dree, Jeff, and Don Jeff, I put into the "family folder." It is full to overflowing. We need to be reminded of the glad and the sad, the exciting and the dull, the hurt and the healing touch. These are the fabric of life and affirm that we have come through.

My eyes get worse daily. What is the plan You have for me in these last years? Having provided such wonderful opportunities for worthwhile living, surely You would not now cast me off. I can't believe, God, You want me to give up all reading and writing. You must want something better than that for me! I go to the hospital for tests today. In a very intense way, my life is in Your hands. That is always true, but now, at my age, not only every day, but every minute. Grant me courage and wisdom.

Lorraine says she has two words for prayer, "Hallelujah" and "Help." Today those are my words, too, God.

Mae

★ ★ ★

Dear God,

The day is bright. Let the sun brighten up my sluggish body and let Your light give understanding and warmth to my spirit.

I go this morning for the "closing" of the house. You must be interested too, for all along, I have felt You were in the background directing the moves. Because of this, I go calmly to Foxwood. Even when I openly express my fear about sufficient funds, deep down, I feel You are in charge and will provide what I need, whether *I* am satisfied or not.

During this long life, there have been heartaches and despair, and I have sincerely longed to die, but as I see it all now, You have been close by. I stand on a hill and look back across the valley at the different sizes and shapes of the farms. They have been plowed and divided into parcels. Such have been the years of my life, broken into sections, torn apart by the flow of circumstances, made barren by the lack of rain of confidence, separated by the fences of envy and competition. Yet, this morning, I give thanks that You have been there during each experience and the backward view gives the appearance of neatness. Continue, Oh God, Your guidance as I enter yet another section of the field to plant.

So this *is* an important year in my life. I might just be moving on my 82nd birthday. How about that! Well, it can be "scary and exciting," as Dree put it. So, "right on!" Be with me, go with me, God, into this new adventure. But, how I hate the thought of being 82! That number could mean nothing to me, if I didn't know the comments of pity and condescension:

"She is 82 and looks well, doesn't she?"

"She is 82 and able to do what she does?"

"She is 82. Don't you think she is too old to be asked?"

"She is 82. I don't think she would be interested."

God, help me to accept 82. You have been so good to me. Help

111

me to let my gratitude drown out all feelings of resentment against society for its attitude. Free me from that attitude myself. I pray for Your glory to live in me. How mixed is that with my own desire to be liked? God, I do try to be obedient to Your will. I do want all with whom I come in contact to know Your grace and glory and love. Yet, sparkling through that, I want people to recognize me as a channel of Your radiance. How, God, do I put these things together in a workable whole? Sometimes, I really don't know how pure my motives are. I have so far yet to go.

May all the contacts I have today be such that Your spirit will be there whispering instructions.

★ ★ ★   Mae

Dear God,

I was so exhausted. I went to sleep last night without any "thank You" or praise for the day. If I am getting any better about connecting my activities with You, then my record before must have been pitiful.

I am in a hurry-flurry mind this morning. Can there be real prayer when I am this way? But what is real prayer, if it is not taking me "just as I am"? Even as I write this, the whirling machine inside settles into a slower, quieter gear.

Word came that I have a ground floor apartment at Foxwood! I don't know why this was so important to me, but learning of it caused me to shout with joy. During this entire time of transition, I have worked at being willing to accept whatever was to be, but at the same time, I felt You were there, keeping an eye on things. Often, it was as if I were on the stage, acting out the role of faith, and Your presence was in the wings saying, "Right on. I need help in accepting all of the kindness of people during these farewell days. Yesterday, Virginia had an open house for me and a host of people came to wish me well, to pray Your blessing upon my move, to say thanks for the contacts we had had. God, I do not understand. I cannot have had such influence. I have just lived. I have tried in speeches to broaden people's horizons, to give a sense of mission. It is all very strange. Is there a way I can show appreciation?

I'm beginning those "last time" occasions. On Monday, the Book Club was here for the last time. Next month, I will have the Canasta Group for the last time. There is something terminal about these months. I have to remind myself that this summer, I will be doing some things for the "first time!"

Now, before You, I remember my friends, the needs of the world, the suffering of others. Let me be conscious of Your presence and Your power.

Beat in my heartbeats.

★ ★ ★

Mae

Dear God,

I'm in bed with the flu today, praying that I can "let go and let God."

Friends continue to be kind. The farewell at Downey had a long line of folks with handclasps, hugs, a few tears and a multitude of words. God, forgive me if I misjudge, but some were so exaggerated . . . but I rejoiced in the showing of affection.

I was invited to the CWF meeting last night. So many people spoke to me so lovingly, that for the first time I really believed them. Before, I thought people were just "being nice," or were doing the proper and gracious thing, because of the occasion. I was really loved last night by a group of wonderful women.

Each day I should have written of the kindnesses shown me. Nobody could understand how I am overwhelmed by it all. Much of it has an unreal feeling about it. I honestly do not see myself in the light others see me. The things they mention (ways I have helped) have not been insignificant, but they have not been noteworthy, either. If I wrote all night, I could scarcely include all of the expressions of appreciation and love on the part of others and my reactions to them. Honestly unbelievable! I am grateful that the Reading Five acceded to my wish that they do nothing special for me. They are a close circle and an emotionally demanding occasion with them is more than I can take right now.

At least I can continue reading when I'm sick. The Old Testament is such a strange book. You seem to be destroying more than creating. You condemn more than You commend. You strike fear into the hearts of Your listeners more than You love. How grateful I am for the New Testament! I have listened to Hans Kung (who is forbidden by the Catholic Church to continue teaching). As I listened, it came to me that the God of the Old Testament had little concern for His enemies, that He disregarded human rights. In the Old Testament, "Vengeance is mine, sayeth the Lord, I will recompense." The New Testament indicates, "Mercy is mine, sayeth the Lord, I will judge." How grateful we are for Jesus, who felt He understood You and told the story of the Prodigal. God, grant me a clearer understanding of Jesus. Make possible a sense of His presence. If this happens, will I know enough to fall on my knees, as the shepherd did?

Back over the years, I have written You often of pain and fear of the future. You have cared for both. They are still there in the wings, ready to rush on stage, but You seem to spot their entrance and they remain in the shadows, while I stand in the center spotlight of Your love. Thank You.

Mae

★ ★ ★

Dear God,

I write that boldly, following our group's conversation yesterday, as to whether You exist. At times, I wonder, too. But all my questions cannot shake my own experience or my judgment, that You *are*. Thank You, God, for You.

I have probably cooked the last real entertainment dinner in this house. I'm tired, but I feel great. Most of the packing is done. People have been kind beyond all imaginings. Things have been said to me about somebody who couldn't have walked the earth in my body. I'm taking all the cards to Foxwood to read one day at a time and then I'll write back to each person. So, in addition to my regular day by day writing, I'll write others, savoring the happiness of the contacts I've had in this community. "Unbelievable" is a constant word in my vocabulary these days.

· ·

Tonight, a whirling storm of feelings fly in gusts around and within. Gratitude that the house is sold to such a nice young couple and with the family helping me move, I am not in this alone. Don Jeff wrote in the last letter, "I'm trying to accept the years at 238, all its memories, the way a house can become an extension of self—my years of growing, the school years, the coming-home times, the planting and painting events. We will both be leaving. I'm just going to let the sad feelings flow, not going to dam them up. I'm glad we will be together, *leaving* and *going* into a new place, for it will be a new home for me, too. *Wherever you are will be home.*" Beautiful!

Composing songs is certainly not my forte, God, but I think you want me to do it (as long as You don't have to hear me sing off-key!), and so, an offering as I leave this place.

A Hymn of Praise

Let me sing my song of praise
Every hour of every day.
For the kindness of His love
Guides and brightens all my way.

'Round about me like the air
I am conscious of His love.
I will ever grateful be
For the care He has for me.

                                        Amen and Amen.

                                                        Mae

                    ★ ★ ★

Dear God,

Yesterday I lay down to nap and there came a knocking at the
door, but before I could get presentable and go to the door, the
person was gone. I might have missed an angel visit—or
somebody selling candy. Of such events are days made.

I am reading Ruth Graham's *Sitting By My Laughing Fire*
again. It was so lovely, so beautiful, so meaningful. How I would
like to have the ability to express my thoughts in such a way.
How I long to know Jesus as she does. Lord, Jesus come to me.
Make Yourself known to me. Can You not come as long as I have
doubts? Only I cannot be sure, so I scurry back to the arms of
God.

"God and I together add to the world's store of love." What a
grand idea! *God* and *I* do it. *Together* we do it, don't we, God?
You are always present to do Your part. It is I who forget so often
(just as I forgot I was to bake the communion bread today).
Forgive me, *we* cannot add to the store of love, when *I* fail to do
my part. I wish I knew how You work. Maybe my part is just to
be grateful. That's certainly not difficult!

I just read a fine interpretation of the Great Commandment:
    "*Faith* is the needed attitude toward You,
    Love, the attitude toward others,
    Hope, the attitude toward myself."

It's Dad's birthday. He was born in 1875. I should write a page of memories of him, but I am too full of the future to write of the past. Foxwood is as good a place, probably far better, as any I have seen in which to spend the last years of life. That's a strange feeling. "The last years of life" sounds like a terminal illness, which it is—terminal. For years I was so sure I would live right here at 238 Ohmer 'til the end, but chances are I'll end life at Foxwood. I don't feel as melancholy as that sentence sounds, God. On the contrary, I am very content with the decision. Together, Don Jeff, Jenny and I made the plans with excitement. The apartment can be as warm and homey as 238. In fact, there is no reason why "the spirit of the pink house" can't be trucked right along with the furniture. Haven't I said all through my life that the important thing is the *attitude* of surroundings, that one takes happiness or unhappiness right along with her? Habits of living and habits of thought *are* dependable. Thank You for this life. It has been rich beyond measure.

While houseguests are here, I will find it harder to keep in touch with You, so You, please keep in touch with me.

Mae

★ ★ ★

Dear God,

On this beautiful May morning, help me to be beautiful-in-spirit. At a time when I needed all kinds of help, I did not find time or take time to write, but I prayed often during the trip, as You know. My heart is full of praise, thanksgiving and gratitude for all those who helped with the move, for Jenny and Don Jeff and all they did, for the beauty of Foxwood and the comfort it provides, for a dedicated and friendly staff, for health and wealth, for faith, hope, love and prayer. Truly, my cup runneth over!

I can finally talk about it, God. As I closed the door on the pink house that morning, a physical pain shot through my body, but it didn't last. I was surrounded by friends saying goodbye. There wasn't a finality about it, as I had feared. How often, how often what we fear or worry about does not happen.

Don Jeff and Jenny have pitched in with strength, cheer and enthusiasm in settling the apartment. The arranging and rearranging would fill pages if I wrote about all of it. But the results are charming. I have never had it so good. The glitter may wear off, but, for now, a good noon meal in a cheerful dining room, a washing machine just down the hall, a disposal in the kitchen, all put me in the lap of luxury. I, who have always preached the simple life style, like having this "forced" upon me.

The kids celebrated my birthday a bit ahead of time with a cake and 10 candles, one for each decade and two to grow on. A pine tree and a hanging flower basket were their "living gifts." My gratitude overflows this day!

Thank You, Thank You. How can I say it? I long for exalted words with which to exalt You, for sacred words to show forth Your uniqueness, for creative words which will proclaim how I am a "new creature" because of Your love!!

Mae

★ ★ ★

Dear God,

The morning is beautiful. The weather is cool, and I sit here like a bump on a log. What is wrong with me that I have no desire to write You? This is the first morning here when I have felt a sense of despair that *this* is to be my *life* from now on. There have been lots of like moments in the past, but I was ready for the unexpected, the surprises of life. But, now . . . the newness and comfort of this place become as ashes and I ask myself, "Why exist?" I do miss keenly, deeply, the services at Downey Ave. Both Sundays, I have been here in body, but mind and spirit and love have been back at Downey. I am filled with longing for old and dear friends, for the familiar—the kitchen sink and white cupboards, for the sound of the floor as I walk from wood to carpet, for the burning bush at the front window and the pink stone porch, for familiar smells and sounds. Oh, God, I am so homesick!

I will manage this eventually, but it is going to take some time and more than a little doing. Be kind and patient, please.

Mae

117

Dear God,

Today I am at Foxwood and I am content! I do not know exactly where along the way You gave the sign, but it must have come through letters from Merle and Tom, the visit we made last November, the selling of my house. Now that I am here, I know it to be the right choice. All the way, You led, but so quietly, I was not aware of it. Now reign in this new house. Let Your Spirit go in the letters I write. I feel I can still be helpful with friends. Help me to make them a source of joy to everyone to whom I write. *Let that be my ministry.*

God, show me how to live here in such a way that I add goodness to others' lives and enrich this place. Help me to know how much I should undertake. There seems no reason why I shouldn't accept assignments—if You are ready to help.

I *am* going to the Quadrennial. The doctor says all is well, but I know, God, it isn't. There are too many fainting spells. Help me to handle them and may they not happen in embarrassing places. Do guide and guard me. Be with the thousands of women getting ready and with all the leaders (*I* especially need help).

Tomorrow, I go to see the eye doctor. Somehow, I think my eye is better. It *is* better. I have been afraid to try it out, but I just did and I see a *lot better!* Thank You that I am able again to see! Deep gratitude for that. My thanks run like a rushing brook, so that by the time I have noticed a floating leaf, another is rushing by and then another and another.

That is Your day, God, and this is my life. Live and move in it.

Mae

★ ★ ★

Dear God,

Thank You for this wonderful time I have had here "back home" again in Indianapolis and for the kindness of the people. Now we make preparations to leave for Michigan and we ask Your blessings for each moment of the trip north.

. . . .

What a blessed day! Here I am at Crystal Lake. It's like the Jews going up to Jerusalem or the Moslems to Mecca. The soloist this morning sang "God Is in Everything." That's easy to believe as I sit here glancing up, now and then, to look out across the lake. Perfect peace. There is a strong wind today. The lake is full of waves with white caps rushing toward the shore. The sky is crystal blue with fluffy-white-fast-moving-clouds racing with the white caps. It is a picture that I will recall whenever I wish.

Spirit of the Living God
  Alive and well in this world
  Creeping into everything from stone to star
  From the newborn to the dying old
  Touching the timid with power
  And the powerful with timidity
  Fall now afresh on me.

Spirit of the Living God
  Melt my indifference to the great needs of the world
  My irritation when I think conversation is trivial
  My frustration when plans fail
  My uncertainty of feelings.

Spirit of the Living God
  Mold me into a vessel of usefulness
  Into a path of righteousness
  Into a neighbor of helpfulness
  Into a medium of Your love.

Spirit of the Living God
  Fill me with faith
  With assurance of Your will
  With a vision of Your kingdom
  With love that does not fail.

Spirit of the Living God
  Use me to show that all are Your children
  To make known Your love
  To encourage others
  To bring joy to daily living
  To be an example of how to grow old.

God, hear my prayer

Mae

★ ★ ★

Dear God,

It is a beautiful, cool, Michigan Sunday afternoon, and Don Jeff and I have had a pleasant, congenial time. I laughed heartily. Thank You for such simple, happy pleasures.

I find myself hesitant to talk of my faith with the grandchildren, or to ask them anything about what they believe. Is that "trusting the process," as Raines says, or is it just being a coward? Help me to turn them over to You. I get so sick of myself at times. I know better. Help, help, help help. Thanks, thanks, thanks, thanks.

I have been to the "Cedars" to see the growth of a house which will surely become a home. The amount of hard, skilled work necessary to produce a log house is tremendous. Watching for an hour gave me an appreciation of house-building which I had not known. Even my own little "house," though not made of logs, has taken on a value that has nothing to do with money. The sawdust paths in the woods are charming. When I first saw them, I felt a surge of emotion, white trails stretching through the dark woods, and a desire to follow each into an enchanted forest.

. . . .

My company has gone. It was so easy for us to live together. We gave each other plenty of space. We met for lunch, and again for dinner and an evening of games. Between meals, each went her own way—to walk, bike, swim, sleep, read or sit quietly on the beach. We have seen no TV, read no newspapers, had no phone calls. We have existed well without any contact with the outside world. It would not be fair to live that way all the time, but this time apart has made it easier, I hope, to return to the world of activity. There has been no fear here. No door has been locked, day or night, house or car. What a comfort to know such is possible, even for a brief time.

I have had periods over these last years, when the death wish was very strong and even though it meant oblivion, I wanted it. Right now, sitting in the sunshine, looking out at the lake, there is only a desire for life and plenty of it. You are so good to me and I am so grateful. Now, as I try harder to sense Your presence, aid me in that. May I "center-in," pay "attention," be patient, be "there," waiting for You to touch me. Use me as an instrument of Your grace. May I return to work and live at Foxwood, with no feeling of haste. May I retain the calmness of the lake and the beauty of the pines. Thank You, God.

Mae

★ ★ ★

Dear God,

It is a beautiful Sunday. It is Your day. Thousands will go to the race track, but thousands will be at church. May Your will be done in each group.

Gratitude overflows this day. What an experience I have had, blacking out and going to the hospital. Thank You for the doctors. Thank You that I am home and the heaviness is gone from my head. How frightening it was not to be in control, and I did not, or could not, remember that You were in charge. But You were. Thank You for Your constant care. Guide me now as I get ready for the Quadrennial. Lead me to read the most helpful books and direct my thinking.

I go to speak to a group on the second floor tomorrow. Speak through me. May I be factual, but interesting. May friendliness be in my voice and love in my actions. Let the true spirit of love reign in this community . . . . Bless all who work to make this true. Thank You especially for Merle and Tom, for Charlie and Floyd, and for all the Foxwood staff.

I have hesitated in these last years to call You "Father," but recently I have come to You as a child, who needs encouragement and cuddling. Thank You for Your softness. I am grateful. "Pull yourself to God, not God to you."

Mostly, it seems, my prayers are intercession when some should be praise and thanksgiving, but You know, God, that I am grateful, that I rejoice in my relationship (not understood, but rewarding) with You. I do not have the divine and heavenly ways to express praise, but I do have the needs of others in mind and I long for their well-being. I seem to know how to think of them, and I believe putting their names before You is of help to them. Now I name them as though "telling my beads." Each one is precious beyond words. . . .

Mae

★ ★ ★

Dear God,

These moments are after lunch, instead of after breakfast. But, regardless of when they come, they are an oasis in the day's activities.

Always, here at the Quadrennial, I have a fear of superficiality, God. I pray for a genuine sense of Your presence. May we not fall into a warm, sentimental, emotional bath of well-being that leaves out the world. I have my doubts about many things and more things I do not understand. "I believe, help Thou my unbelief." What I need most is some way to let others know, some way that makes sense to them. I cannot *prove* anything, and yet the conviction needs to come through. I pray most earnestly that I may be able to put Mae Ward in the background and that You will speak through me to the great company of women. This is a time of gratitude and thanksgiving for all who provide information, inspiration, and entertainment. Great rest to all who are here. A special thanks for the many friends who spoke words of love and courage.

In this great gathering, I wonder how You feel about the world. Are You interested in royal weddings as well as the poor of Haiti? I find it so hard to include the world in thought and prayer. It seems to me that if I deal with Foxwood and the family, scattered here and there, I have used up my capacity for concern. What walls am I supposed to build or expected to rebuild? Nehemiah was so sure, so dedicated, but even he had only one objective— the walls of Jerusalem. What should be my Jerusalem? Argentina with its destruction of human rights? Africa with its starving children? Our nation, with greed in ascendancy? How? Where? What?

I had a dream, God. I feel some uneasiness with it. I went out in the hills to take a walk. It got dark. I heard friends coming and one of them said, "We must find her before it gets too dark." I didn't want to be found. It was pleasant to be alone. I took a short-cut down the hill. It was hardly a path, but I knew it well! Grant me, I pray, the peace that passeth understanding.

Mae

★ ★ ★

Dear God,

This morning, I give thanks—for a wonderful, long night of sleep with air-conditioning—for an attractive apartment and food—for the amount of sight I have, help me keep it—for letters from friends—for friends who so enrich life—for Downey Ave. and Madison Ave. and Raymore*—for the leadership of the National office—for this time of quiet and thought of You—for Jesus Christ and His influence in the world.

The doctor said I would be unable to see to read or write in a year, but I am still doing it. I know You have worked a miracle with my eyes and I long to shout it to the world, but I have felt You saying, "That is our secret." I don't understand why but Jesus said to some whom He healed, "Tell no one," and I feel You have said that to me. My healing seems to be proof of prayer. Take away any feeling that *my* prayer is the power. Keep me ever conscious that my prayer is only the flipping of the switch. Let me leave things with You and be content. I can pragmatically say, "Most decisions are out of my hands anyway," but I want to believe and say, "All things are in the hands of God," and really turn over to You the outcome.

The sun shines bright this day. The out-of-doors looks like poetry read aloud. The sun shines on the mirror. It shows up a smudge never visible when the sun is not on it. So my life looks pretty good until Your light shines on it, and shows it for what it really is. It's spiritual Windex time, God. Rub gently.

How personal or individualized is the statement, "Knock and it shall be opened to you"? May I knock for others, or does that interfere with their own self will? Well, I am knocking anyway for good health for the following . . . .

Mae

---

*Three local churches that played a large part in Mae's life.

Dear God,
The day begins hurried and hot. I shall go to church and seek quiet and coolness. (We have air-conditioning.)

....

I'd like to reminisce, God—to remember a happier time. In my teens, this was an afternoon for nut hunting. The youth of Madison Ave. would gather on the steps of the church with baskets for the chestnuts, hickory nuts and black walnuts we would find. The chestnuts were the favorites. They could be cracked with our teeth. Dad was always on hand to lead off. He would have taught the men's Sunday School class and preached in the morning. He had an evening sermon ahead, but he was ready for a hike with the young people. It was about a mile from the church to the hills. This was covered fast, for we were eager to start climbing, walking through the fallen leaves (how they rustled) to the nut trees. Someone was always calling out, "Let's go this way. I know where the trees are." As we went, couples paired off. "Dating" was not permitted by many parents (until 17 or 18), so Sunday afternoon on a church hike, overseen by Brother Yoho, was an exciting time to let a boy help you over a big rock or up a steep grade. Holding his hand for a little bit longer than necessary was a daring, fun experience. It was on such a day that Norm and I realized there was something special between us. It had been reported to me the previous Sunday that he had said, "I think I'll marry the preacher's daughter." I thought that a good joke, but still that Sunday afternoon, I liked the touch of his hand. I don't recall if we brought home any nuts!

Thank You for the goodness of friends. Help me not to be a stingy receiver, but to rejoice in the kindness of others, not thinking always of how I can repay them. Yesterday, I did a pretty good job of "being present." I almost failed, but recovered. Thank You. Shall we try again?

Mae

★ ★ ★

Dear God,

I know it helps to have these moments, though sometimes I think You might be saying "There she is again." I do believe it is of value to write my thoughts to You each day. Do You think it is of value? As I compare it with writing Don Jeff, I know it's great importance to complete living. I wish You could write back. You do, but I don't always know it. You must have "written back" last night with the complete cessation of pain. But it puzzles me, God, that if You can heal it, why does the pain come on in the first place? The result of Natural Law? Which You, being Maker of Laws, cannot break? How wonderful You are and how little I understand.

God, is it OK for me to act "as if I were the only one," or is it better to not bother You with the "minor things of life"? I fear I will go on bothering You. Through all the years, You have been there, encouraging me, but I am such a slow learner. I am retarded in spiritual thinking, but not in offering hymns of praise. Accept my humble offering as You overlook my short- comings.

> Let me sing praises to You
> in my heart, all the day long
> I will sing praises to You
> with my voices in these
> Moments of the morning
>
> Thanking You for the
> pleasantness of this day
> Grateful that You are in
> control of my life
>
> Thankful for the goodness
> of people who make possible
> these attractive surroundings
> Rejoicing that You are always present
>
> Giving thanks that You have
> given me family and friends
> Praising You and Your
> loving kindness forever.

Mae

Dear God,

You know how I am overwhelmed with fear of the nausea and the blackouts, the fear of not being able to function. I want to turn it *all* over to You. I want to feel that You will be the guide, that all I need to do is give it to You. I wish so much I would be sure, but as I wrote last year, my faith is delicate and fragile, like the retina of my eye. I want to run to You and hide my head in Your lap. I want You to put Your hand on my head and tell me "Everything is OK. Don't worry."

Do others have pain constantly as I have? They bear theirs so cheerfully. I keep thinking there must be relief, but there is none. These "letters" are becoming a "health report." But what can I do? "Even though our physical being is gradually decaying, yet our spiritual being is renewed day after day" (2 Cor. 4:16, TEV). So true. I am never free from pain these days, but after an hour each morning, my spirit is renewed.

> Great God
> > Almighty God
> > > God the Lover
> > > > God the Creator
> > > > > God the Keeper of my soul

> Look upon me this morning
> > Bringing thanksgiving to You
> > > Calling upon You for strength and guidance

> God of the Universe
> > God of all People
> > > God of little children and
> > > > God of sinners

> Hear me as I call to You for courage to endure.

May my daily involvement in the world be my worship offered to You.

Mae

★ ★ ★

★ ★ ★

Dear God,

I want to write "dearest" God, but there is only one God, so I guess You *can* be the "dearest." I am so grateful for this time when I put before You the activities of the day, my concern for friends, for the needy of the world. What does it mean to be a child of Yours in our world? To be able to turn to You in every moment?

1. To be honest with myself.
2. To be concerned about others.
3. To find joy with other followers of Christ.
4. To believe that good will eventually win out.
5. To be assured of future contact with You.
6. To feel I am co-creator with You in making relationships good.
7. To find cause for optimism in all this.

I would give a sacred meaning to a commercial phrase, "Reach out and touch someone." It causes me to see my fingers in a way not seen before, and sets my mind wandering. How often have they been used aright? How often have they been used, to touch a hand, or prepare a dish, to play the typewriter keys and bring a song to a lonely heart, to hold a cup of wine and a piece of bread, to fold in quiet supplication?

In the workshop, I said, "Prayer cannot change God's purpose, but it can release it. It does not change God's intention, but it does change His action!" Is this too presumptuous, God? May I not just send "urgent telegrams of prayer" to You, but seek for genuine communication.

Mae

P. S. Why is it so hard for men today to have an interest in the spiritual life and yet most of the "saints" are men? Doesn't it go back again to education, opportunity and biological freedom? Raise up great women, Oh God, so that there will be equality among the saints in the coming generations.

1982

Dear God,
    May I wish You a Merry Christmas, God—but then *every one* has been, hasn't it?
    The softly falling snow caused me to imagine myself a snowflake—so briefly to live, but able to give the spot where I fall a bit of beauty, so vulnerable to any passing footstep, which could destroy me, but able to water the ground and be the source of life.
    The news has just said, "Never before have the decorations in the White House been so elaborate." Dear God, how can they do that when the numbers of poor become greater every day? What am I doing that is equal or similar to the White House for which I need to ask forgiveness and make a change in my way of living and giving?
. . . .
    It was a beautiful, joyful service, God. Words tumble out in gratitude . . .

It's Christmas Sunday.
    Snow on the ground
    Sun in the sky
    Ham in the oven
        smelling good.
    Friends expected
        bringing cheer.
    Realizing I am who I am, by the grace of God.
    Claiming the past with gratitude
        Anticipating the future with hope.
    Rejoicing in all that surrounds me
        Conscious that much is required.
    Living in the spirit of love for all.
    Working in the sight of God.

It's Christmas Sunday.
    The last advent candle has been lit.
    The candle of love.
    Love which really makes the world go 'round
        For, without this love,
        The Universe, would or could, come to a stop.
        Well, that can't be quite true.
    But it must be true that if God got His fill of
        Humanity and its lack of love
        He could destroy it, as He did Sodom and
Gomorrah.
    But He won't, because He still hopes
        That the world will accept His gift of love.

The sun shines beautifully and I hope it is in Your plan to warm up the world!

Mae

9

1983

"Today I feel like a tadpole in a little pond, wondering if this is all there is."

Dear God,

I start another book of letters to You. This is a good thing I do! I would like to make it a book of *Praise, Thanks, and Gratitude,* and these sentiments will always be a part of each day's expression of thoughts. I will also go on writing time and again of my anxieties, my fears, my needs. I am Your child, who comes full of "I want," so I am filled with requests for Your help in countless areas. As before, no doubt, both the "Thank You" and the "Please" will be mixed up together.

Mae

Dear God,

This seems like a good place to rendezvous with You, but it doesn't seem to work out as well as it did at 238 Ohmer. Right now, I feel pretty ineffective, yet I go on accepting invitations to speak, since I believe these are Your concerns. But before I go to speak, I must deepen my own spiritual life. I feel so sleepy. I do not function with full alertness. It must be due to all the medication. I would like to drop taking it, but would that be wise?

I am surrounded by illness here, much more than I expected. Seldom a day passes that someone is not taken to the hospital, never a week that I do not hear the siren of the ambulance. The touch of love is constantly needed, Your compassion and concern, imperative. Be present with all the sick, weary and discouraged.

Ira's meditation has prompted me to look back:

Through the clouds of loss . . .
    a mother I can't remember,
    a father who died at 64,
    a little daughter at the age of two
    a husband by divorce when I was 40.

Through the clouds of pain . . .
    six major operations.

Through the clouds of fear . . .
    loss of vision,
    a long, painful exit from life.

But, through the clouds, there have *always* been glimpses of God
And a sense of certainty that He cares!

Don and Jenny move today. Bless them in "The Cedars." May its walls see many happy years and its roof continue to provide shelter for blessings as You have provided for all of us in the past.

Today, may I be a co-creator with You, in bringing happiness to others.

Mae

★ ★ ★

Dear God,

Good morning. How does the world look to You today? I have sung hymns with gladness this day. A tiny dish of sun shine fell on the wall and held me enthralled. It was, in reality, a miniature round rainbow. I longed for someone to share it with. The same emotion I'd had upon seeing the Northern Lights: "Oh, come and see what the Lord has done." You came into this small room this morning. Let my life, this day, reflect a small, shining circle of Your love.

Thank You for the work of the staff in giving such lovely recognition to volunteers. Thank You for the spirit of this community and the general spirit of helpfulness. •Help me in whatever should be my part. Thank You for the tulips blooming outside my window, for the little tree waiting to be planted, for the beauty of spring and the joy of friendship. With all of this, I find myself reaching out and longing for the family, friends and community of faith at Downey Ave. How marvelously has my life been blessed.

Thank You for Harold's letter and his meditations on St. Francis. More of us ought to be straightforward about our personal experiences, for through them we help others. I remember before You now, the friends of Indianapolis. The names and faces come faster than I can write . . .

Be present in me in a vital way, as I speak at Vespers. Give me strength and grace. May what I say ring honest and true.

Today, I help in the health center, and I don't want to go. Nevertheless, I go and ask for Your presence with all of the sick. So many are in such a sad condition. Death would be so welcome. Enable me to be of help so that we all may "live."

Journey with me, please.

Mae

* * *

Dear God,

Such a devastating thing happened yesterday at Country Club Church. You know all about it, but why wasn't I permitted to end the session? I was so frightened. I don't know what happened. The blackout came while I was still speaking. What must they think? No doctor, no medicine can cause me to function, only You. Should I accept any other engagements? How can I now? Will it happen again? It does no good to dwell on it, so help me to throw it off and get on with living.

I feel so uncertain about the "what" and the "why" of these years. I am puzzled about how to sort out values. I always thought that life should be of worth and value to the end, but it wasn't so for Dee. It isn't for a lot of folks here. It may not be for me. I want to have faith. I want always to be grateful, to trust, to love. Never have I needed Your guidance more. *Never* have I been so unsure as to how to sort things out and make choices. *I need You now.*

. . . .

Another death by stroke. She had no waiting. Death came quickly. Thank You for her life and welcome her home. Her death made me so conscious of the future and what I ought to do to avoid being a burden for a long period of time. Show me how to live each day well and, in accord with Your will, to experience each minute to the fullest.

If letters are to be my method of service, help me to be sensitive to the peculiar needs of each person and guide me as I write. Let my "letter prayers" not be too few, too little, or too late.

Mae

★ ★ ★

Dear God,

I am like a child eager to tell the parent of the excitement of the party. Pouring out, words tumbling over one another to convey the surprise and delight of the occasion. And so, dear God, I come rushing to You this morning eager to tell You of all that has happened and is expected to happen.

How difficult life is. One hour I feel great and the next strange feelings go through my body, my eyes blur, my head seems to swell and there is a tingling in my ankles. If I cannot get to a chair, I know I will fall. After the blurring passes and the feelings stop, I feel tired, the back of my neck is stiff and I feel sleepy. Someday, I expect I will lose consciousness and the future will be more uncertain still. I write this, God, so I can clarify my thoughts in Your presence, so that all may be laid before You.

Didn't you grow disgusted with me? I debate within myself as to whether I want to be well or not. It goes like this:

I: I don't want to live too many years.

Me: But you enjoy living.

I: I am afraid of years of slow death.

Me: True, but there is a basic faith that somehow God will *not* let that happen.

I: I have no right to believe I'll get preferential treatment.

Me: That is true, but somehow, you believe the end won't be so bad.

I: Today, the sun shines, the tulips bloom and my body has little pain, so I will rejoice and be glad.

Me: Good, then let go and let God.

What about "faith"? Do we have more or less of it as we grow older? I feel the quality of its changes. When I was younger, I believed that faith could *remove* mountains. Now I believe that faith shows me the way to go *around* them.

I have the task ahead of writing the prayers for a study book.* Help me, God. Help me even to make a start and not put it off. I need Your thoughts. How do You want to be approached—as Almighty God, as a Father/Mother? May I be able to put myself in the place of those who will read, and write in the way that will have meaning for them. Continue to challenge me!

Let me use my eagerness to write others as a ministry for You. As I write, give the words to be helpful. In spite of my own feelings and stumblings of body and spirit, may my concern help others rise up and run without weariness!

Mae

★ ★ ★

*Prayer, A Way of Life. CWF Group Study for 1984-1985, by Evelyn Hale. Christian Board of Publication, 1984.

★ ★ ★

Dear God,

I know you are powerful and could crush me, as I can step on a bug, but I am not a bug but Your child, and for that I give deep thanks. After steering away from calling You "Father," it seems this morning like the right word to describe our relationship.

The person who called in the middle of the night has warped values. He needs help. May someone touch him today who can be of service. Thank You for the safety of this place and that after the call I could go back to sleep. May I forget and put anger aside.

Life looms so difficult when I do not know the reason for the pain. Last night in the silence of the church, in the solitude of the sanctuary, I felt peace. I rejoiced. I know the blessings of this place and the glorious knowledge that my eyes still serve. Yet this morning, I am a petulant child, whimpering and complaining. Father, give me the will to live graciously, rising above the pain. As You can see, much of my concerns are about my physical body. I ought to be concerned about all the weak spots in my spiritual life. I am, but they are not so localized.

I haven't made any progress during the years of feeling the presence of Jesus. Why can't I? For I do believe You are the living God, and Jesus is Your Son. He is my Savior because I know You through and because of Him. Is that enough, God? I don't think it is. Grant to me a more conscious sense of Christ. This is *the* weak spot in my faith. I do not want to be envious of others, but I long for the assurance of their faith. I hold out my hands ready to be filled. I urge others to, for I feel it is possible, but fail myself.

The new patio garden is truly "amazing grace." Thank You for the vivid expression of the kids' thoughtfulness and love. It will provide endless hours of delight.

Last night I taped the week's meditations for Foxwood. I prayed as I began each. I do not know if they are well done or according to Your will, but I tried!

I'm going to learn how to play pool today! Doesn't that surprise You?

Mae

Dear God,

The world is beautiful. The grass grows greener by the minute. The trees take on a haze of green. The tulips' tightly closed buds appear and this physical body responds with a burst of strength.

How does a child receive the Kingdom? Almost thoughtlessly. As a parent says, "Let's go to the zoo," and the child goes. Seldom does she ask, "Why?" The child goes with expectations, willing and eager for surprises, sure it will be a good experience. Is Jesus saying, "Park your logic at the door. Come in with the belief that what will happen will be good . . . . Don't analyze. Just come in."?

Am I doing the right thing in going to Michigan for the summer? I need You through this strangle-tangle time of physical reactions, as new and strange sensations take over in my body. I would rather be sick *here,* if illness is in store. "Though I walk through the valley of the shadow of death, Thou art with me." I do not mind death. I welcome it in preference to suffering or inactivity. God, help me to live the Psalm and not just write it.

How difficult it is to watch a body lose strength, for a body full of energy and health is a thing of beauty. Joy comes from watching the human body when it is well developed and under control, like watching Jeff vault; but there is a certain distaste, a withdrawal, when the body of another fails. I don't want to feel this way. I don't want others to withdraw when my body grows old and disfigured, yet that will be a natural reaction.

This is a bittersweet time of life, God.

Mae

★ ★ ★

★ ★ ★

Dear God,

My pilgrimage has reached a plateau. I am on the edge of the lake. I feel nervous that it looks so far across, but I'm sure it has to be crossed. I have but a small canoe with a paddle. So I am in this frail body with only the paddle of prayer to move me across the choppy waters of the day. Without anxiety, I should continue to paddle, dip left, dip right, until once again, the canoe is carried by the force of my action. It is hard for me to lift the paddle and the lake looks so far across. Are You here in the slow-moving craft of my body? I'm so eager for You to energize me, but it is prayer which will get me across. *My belief in prayer is based on the certainty that You are working for me, with me and in me!* I've had too many experiences to doubt it!!

Let me work with You this morning. What nerve! Yet Jesus taught us to pray, and Paul said, "Keep praying." That prayer opens channels for Your power seems like sheer foolishness, but I go ahead doing it, thinking that it is possible.

Literally dozens of names and faces come before me now and I am eager to remember them—the people who live in this wing and those who have gone, the people I have met in retreats, the Spiritual Companions, the young folks at Downey Ave., people to whom I write, the family. Thank You that I still see. Help me to remember that intercession does not take the place of action on my part, but leads me to take *direct responsibility.*

Here I am, year after year, struggling with the thought of Jesus as my *personal* Savior. Last night I listened to a minister of the Moral Majority. He is so sure that the only way to Heaven is belief in Christ as a personal Savior. If so, what are You going to do with the Jews? Are You the God of vengeance of the Old Testament or the God and Father of the New Testament? I don't see how You can be both? Have You changed or been misrepresented? What are You doing with people like me who would like to believe. Certainly You do not want me to pretend what I do not feel . . . . Some of us need to be straightened out. But who?

Your questioning partner in prayer,

Mae

137

★ ★ ★

Dear God,

Today is the first day of spring. As the earth softens, may I soften my critical thoughts of others; as the new leaves come and the daffodils push through the ground, may a spirit of hope arise within me; as flowers brighten the lawns, may beauty be evident in my life.

Help me to take my own preaching to heart. In my time with You, I *must* be honest. It is painful to hear myself express hostility about others, to deal with greed and guilt and especially to dredge up the fears for the future, but how else can I clear the way for Your presence to enter? How can I *hear* the truth, if I cannot *tell* the truth? It may be painful for us both, God, but I'll do my best to level with You.

I list my blessings with thanks and praise:

—Sight, hearing, movement of body. (I continue to write with deformed fingers, but I see what I write.)

—Great concern and interest in my neighbors and a growing love for them.

—The love of the family.

—The "Maezing Grace" garden.

—Foxwood, its opportunities for good living, and its staff.

—A great letter from Janet.

—Friends, particularly those in Indianapolis.

—An electric typewriter.

—Books of such variety.

—A sense of Your love and presence.

—And more blessings than I can count.

Devotions today have been hit and miss. But on my morning walk, I *sang* praises to You.

Your "off-key" servant,

Mae

★ ★ ★

138

Dear God,

My body absorbs medicine, regulating my heart, but making me dizzy. My spirit absorbs Your presence, giving me peace, but stirring me to indignation about the injustice in the world. TV brings the pain so close and one is bombarded with awful images . . . . The personal pain of women—what would it be like to be beaten by a husband? It is unthinkable. I never saw my father strike anybody. I never saw Norm strike anyone. If he had, I wonder how I would have reacted. God, Your help, Your presence, Your care for all women and children who are abused.

I think back to a young woman I met a year ago in the hospital who had an abortion. I hope life is better for her and that You are touching her. How do You feel about abortion? Surely You are able to take the "soul" of the unborn child into Your care and deal with it tenderly, so that its "real being" is reserved. It could be planted in another situation, where it would be wanted and loved.

God, are You on the side of the nuclear freeze? Nobody tells about our responsibility to the world and how we might act as a *Christian* nation. Of course, we are not, so why don't, or can't, we think from a humanitarian point of view? We seem as if our total concern as a nation is that of survival. What would happen if we put concern for others first? We are *not* ready for the coming of the Kingdom or willing to work for it. Forgive our collective failure. I am deeply sorry to have done so little, for I do not think I leave the world a better place for having passed this way. I wonder how failed, insensitive or ignorant I am in other areas of life. There is still so much to learn and so little time left. God, don't You give us another chance?

I wonder what You think of the film *Oh, God.* I believe You would like it. As a Christian, I wish it could more emphatically make use of Christ and His Lordship, but films are made for money; *that* idea would have offended Jesus.

Thank You for whoever sent the stamps. May they know I am grateful and may I truly "minister through letters."

Mae

★ ★ ★

Dear God,

How do I approach You today? You are the Creator, the Almighty. I rejoice in all I see about me and marvel at the laws of nature. But I find myself coming back to the personal, thinking of You as Love, love which cares.

God, most people seem to believe in *You* in vague, general ways and don't grasp that the only way You can deal with *us* is as individuals. "Let us draw near to the throne with boldness."

La Palabra Diaria suggests that I start the day with statements of affirmation:

I am a child of the All-Powerful.

I am wise. I recognize God within me.

I am confident. The power of God makes me able to manage all that comes into my life today.

I am happy. The peace of Christ is mine, or *Mi vida es feliz, satisfactoria y completa.*

I am content. I am glad I am where I am. I like what I do.

All of the above is true for this day. "Sufficient unto the day is the good thereof." [sic!]

Thank You for Dree's card. Let me now think of Dree and bring to You her life, ability and beauty. Guide her into using all for the best. May she continue to grow in sensitivity and ability to serve. Be with her in her work that she may be honest and understanding of folks. Use her concern for others to bless each group she lives among. Oh, God, let these prayers for her be a force for good, a way in which I can be helpful to her. I go on to think of Jeff—capable, intelligent, with great potential. May he come through the pole vaulting without injury. He has such opportunities. May he choose the right ones.

I enjoy my letter writing career and yet I weary of it, too. But this has happened before, when there is a season of "burn-out." Experience has taught me, "This too shall pass."

Give me patience,

Mae

★ ★ ★

★ ★ ★

Dear God,

When I finally turned my petitions into letters, God, I had not imagined how they would help me "center-in," and how it would "enable" me to have a running conversation with You *all day.*

Another year has passed. In some ways, it has been a strange year, but this morning of my 83rd birthday, I feel great. I thank Thee that the habit of constant conversation grows easier each day. I really do believe *all* thought can be conversation with You.

Help me to accept my age. But I don't accept it, God. It's just that I don't want people making a fuss over it. Help me to be gracious about it. Why do people say to me in various ways, very seriously, "How old are you, really?" "Are you getting along OK?" or even, "Are you able to cope?" Is it because I do better than I am expected to do at this age, or do I show my age in such a way as to cause concern? How am I expected to answer them? Do they think I am pretending when I say I am OK? I could ask them, but would I get an honest answer?

I was remembering today . . . the big book of Bible stories that Dad used for bedtime reading . . . being baptized at the age of 12 in the Ohio River. It was *cold.* I did expect to be made "good" after that and was so disappointed when, within a few days, I told a lie. I blamed *You* for letting *me* do it . . . . Then at 16, I wanted to be a missionary. They were the most exciting people I knew. I thrilled to their stories. I can admit that the real missionary work was, as a whole, disappointing. I had romanticized it. However, when I gave it up, it was a blow . . . the divorce, I felt You had deserted me . . . Dad died the year before . . . then a direct gift from You, a job at the Missions Building. My colleagues were angels in disguise, gracious, loving people. It was then I began again my daily talks with You. I know now, I was NEVER forsaken.

I listened to my TV meditation this morning on "grace" and it was good. You are the loving Father to me. You keep welcoming me into Your presence. Help me to stay there. The idea of the meditation came from You, of that I am confident. I sign off on my 83rd birthday, with Love.

Mae

Dear God,

I need to put foremost this time of writing You. I need to pray in "prime-time." There is a time for eating and entertaining and having my hair done. Why is it so hard to take the time to bring all these things and more before You?

Never can I remember having so much rain, but it makes the nights so deliciously cool for sleeping.

Thank You that I am getting on with the letter writing. Show me how to pass on my love and faith in You. Guide this particular ministry and help me to be alert.

Last year, there was some depression in the loss of daily contact with friends in Indianapolis. Now I am so content. With all of the illness, it has been a good year. I have found my niche. I am accepted and, I hope, loved. Help me to get to know people and to care for them.

Earnestly, two years ago, many of us asked that health be given to Kathleen, and it was not. Often I have prayed for the death of terribly ill friends and they live. So I have plenty of illustrations that my prayers are not in accord with Your will. But Bill's eyes and mine still function and that has to be in response to many prayers, for the doctors have prophesied the opposite.

So ends another year of life with its changes and its good ending!

I rejoice in the family
in the church
in my friends
in this, my new home
in health
in a mind that works, even though it forgets
in my faith and prayer
and their power to make life good.

Thanks be to You, my God, for guidance and countless blessings.

Now we begin anew, You and I. Let's get on with it.

Mae

★ ★ ★

★ ★ ★

Dear God,

Augustine said, "God loves us, every one, as though there were but one of us to love." If I did not believe this, I would miss, daily, a sense of Your presence. When I do not pray, both of us lose, God.

You know that I get upset after a physical and learning from the doctor that I have had a slight stroke, not very damaging, but probably a prophecy of the future. Be with me. Help me to act as a faithful Christian, no matter what happens. I do pray for a death not too lingering and painful. I'm beginning to believe that death may be only incidental and prayer have nothing to do with it. This year, six dear friends have gone from us. May they all be rejoicing in rich new experiences. Thank You for their love.

I think of how I see, even better than last year, and my gratitude is like a flood. That makes me think of the many homeless people and wonder if they can be hopeful and still cope. My own lot is so comfortable. I do give thanks again and again for Foxwood Springs, for family, friends, church, health. It is hard to understand why so many suffer, while so many have it so good, when those who suffer deserve equally the good things. The problem of evil is always with me. Certainly it has always been with You.

Go with me to Spanish class. May we not only study but gain in understanding of one another and realize the value of human contact.

Oh, yes, I have been asked to allow my name to be put up for the Foxwood Springs Board. I think it is a board with more authority than I want to handle. What do You think?

God, You "restoreth my soul," but only when I come to You for restoration!

Mae

Dear God,

I've read a book on being honest with you. I've had no trouble knowing You know *everything* about me:

—how at sea I am sometimes

—how proud I am, which includes being proud of being a child of God

—how I have sinned and not been sorry, for it didn't seem like a sin

—how I fib a little sometimes for no reason at all, except to make a good story better

—how I hurt people by refusing their gifts, because I do not want to be under an obligation to them

—how I would like to "make-over" my best friends

—how grateful for my life and all the opportunities I have had and now, the opportunity to be at Foxwood

—how I appreciate and crave the love of youth

Be merciful with my honesty, God.

I play "Pussie wants a corner." I dash from corner to corner for security, wondering what I will meet during the dash, another loss of awareness, another black-out, another stroke and yet, I am not as fearful of the future as I once was. There is comfort here at Foxwood. I do not want to live too long. I do so "want to go home before dark" and yet my mind seems more willing to accept the dire conditions which surround the exit from this life. This morning, my fingers are so stiff, I can scarcely hold this pen, but I am able to see what I write—for that I am so grateful.

I wish with all my heart, God, I could just relax and let each day care for itself, that I could trust completely that the future belongs to You. But submission has not been my role. I have tried to be responsible and intentional about living. Now I find myself pushed back and forth, up and down by events and my reaction to them. Let Your grace descend upon me!

Thank You that the drivers test is over and I am free to drive. A great load has been lifted from me. A car is so important. With it, I have freedom and mobility, two things I have *never* been without. Help me to use both, to be of service to those who are without.

Mae

★ ★ ★

Dear God,

Thank You for the pleasant, safe trip to Michigan. Thank You for a wonderful Sunday with a marvelous message and beautiful concert last night. It is a wonder, wonderful place to be and my heart overflows with gratitude.

As usual, the cottage was ready to receive me. The blessing of adult, considerate children is beyond any expression in words. The thought that went into preparation for my arrival—flowers in the bedroom; open, empty drawers to receive my things; empty hangers in the closet; a small dresser light turned on, and on the table, a welcome note with suggestions for afternoon activities . . . . I arrived tired, tired, but every touch of the house welcoming me took away, no, lessened, the weariness. Such blessings!

Bay View Bulletin, Sunday, July

Think deeply
Speak Gently
Laugh often
Love much

Work hard
Give freely
Pray earnestly
and be kind

Amen.

Mae

Editor's note: Mae was with us, vacationing in northern Michigan, for the full month of July, 1983. Her sudden passing away at Foxwood Springs came just two weeks after she left us.

During our time together, we gardened, attended lectures, concerts, and evening vespers at Bay View. She had her dearest friends as houseguests, delighted in the visit and maturity of Dree, her granddaughter, and reveled in the athletic achievement at the World University Games (on TV) of her grandson, Jeff.

We read aloud, as we always did. Often, on hearing an incident that struck her as funny, she would laugh until the tears came. She walked the paths through the deep woods with only the dog as her companion and enjoyed her daily devotions on the deck in the early morning sun. "I can pray in this beautiful, beautiful spot," she said, "without ceasing." It was a time of reflection and retreat. It was a time to gather strength for what lay ahead, for we know now that she had had a glimpse of the future. During this period, Mae remained constant in her habits and disciplined in her worship. She gave herself to living fully, sharing her daily faith and her fears with the only one in whom she had absolute trust, her God.

Dear God,

The heat is awful and rain is needed so badly. Can't the law of nature work in such a way that rain may come? The crops need it and loss of crops will work hardship this winter. I am so blessed to be here in this comfortable log house which remains cool. Let Your grace fall upon us.

I also give great, overflowing thanks that I have been able to go to Foxwood and maintain my independence. I am so blessed. May I be worthy of all You do for me and somehow live it out moment by moment. Forgive me for the impatience which comes upon me and for the fear in the night when I realize my heart is racing. Be my guide.

I am so blessed with family and friends. How gracious and beautiful Dree is, in so many ways. Do grant her health and opportunities for service, and may Your presence always be known to her. "The Cedars" is so beautiful, God. Thank You for the creative minds You have "gifted," for the kids and the sweetness of their spirits. Bless them in their endeavors. Let Your grace rest on the three of us sleeping under this roof tonight. Guide us in our love and understanding of each other.

Now I have read the lecture on Gandhi, who said, "God is, though all deny it. Truth is, though none support it"!

The Bay View lecture series on "TV in Society" was so interesting. Help me to remember some of the facts, like 22 commercials to a football game. It is so good to have the chance to hear all of these lectures and stir up the brain cells and enlarge my horizons. I am so grateful that my mind functions. The Lord is with me, what more should I ask?

My heart reels with information. My heart overflows with gratitude. The speakers are so good and helpful. The friendship of friends is so heart-warming. I am so blessed. Grace was so gracious and the group of women gathering for Bible study, so sincere. Guide each one.

My understanding of prayer, as the ultimate communication, is so limited. Like the disciples, I plead, "Teach me how to pray." But one thing I know, prayer is essential to life, so I'll stumble on, asking that You accept my childish attempts to relate. How obvious it is. If we will find *You,* we must seek *You,* we must call *You. You* are not an abstract noun or a learned phrase, like "Ground of Being." *You* are a personal God, and *I will come to You.*

Mae

Dear God,

Thank You for a wonderful night of sleep—for this beautiful place, for the thoughtfulness of Jenny. May her blithe spirit continue on its merry way. Thank You for a deep well to water the trees, for books to read, for health and medicine, for this time in which to think, pray and write. Let Your grace descend upon all trying to do Your will.

I need to do something to share all of this bounty. How? Where? Help me to retain a great deal of this week, so I can pass it on for the good of others and the coming of the Kingdom. I shall try to write more letters to influence people in high places.

Now I sit in this lovely living room of "The Cedars," enjoying its quiet and calm. It isn't going to be easy to go back to Foxwood, yet I like it and know it is the place for me. I thank You for it. Help me to make my life of worth, wherever I am. Increase my faith and my ability to live in love, growing in my understanding of the Christian way and putting it into practice.

I am grateful for reading aloud books like *Rolling Thunder.** Is it possible to be in touch with the Great Spirit in such a way that Rolling Thunder can work miracles? I believe it is possible! But, what about the starving people who need food? What can the relationship be between need and the person? You and Your laws? There were lots of needy folks when Jesus lived, but He took care of only a few. We are all Your creatures. Are there "favorites"? Or are the ones like Rolling Thunder in closer touch with You and Your will? Questions, questions, questions.

My heart and mind join in praise and thanks.

Mae

★ ★ ★

Rolling Thunder, by Doug Boyd. Delta Books, 1974.

Dear God,

This is my last day at "The Cedars." It has been a lovely, never-to-be-forgotten time. Thank You for this *special* blessing. May this place be a continuing haven of peace and beauty.

I am curious, God. How do Jenny and Don Jeff see me? I seem to myself to be the same, but what to them? I probably talk too much. At times, I am argumentative. I bring the past up too often. Help me in my decision to leave the past to the past. The time never comes, it seems, when one really lets children go. Being a parent is a life-long job , a rewarding job, but at times very puzzling, and, for me, *very* satisfying.

Somehow, I am anxious to get this vacation over now and get back to Foxwood.

I am such a strange mixture of emotions, trying to bring my various selves together into a harmonious whole, in which You can move and bring me to a Oneness, so to face the days ahead . . . .

Grant safe travel, I pray.

Mae

July, 1983—Mae and her son, Don Jeff, in front of the newly-completed "Cedars," a log home in northern Michigan, a few days before her death.

Dear God,

I'm having a hard time paddling myself across the lake today. The temperature is so high. My blood pressure is up. I feel so listless. In Michigan, I felt good. Here I want to sit or lie down. Before I start to read anything, help me figure out why I feel this way. All of the time I was with the kids, I had only one dizzy, feeling-faint spell. I got one here yesterday, and again this morning. It has been constant with a bad headache. I think back on how I went to lectures day after day, watered young trees and hiked in the woods, feeling good, eager for learning and life. This morning I do not care. Even writing this to You is an effort. What advice do You have? How *many* times I've thought the end was coming with breast cancer, lung cancer, uterine cancer, and I'm still here. I need Your care and help again—as I have needed and received it in the past.

Thank You for the helpful people on this hall, and for Velva who took me to the hospital yesterday. May the Doctor be on the right track. It's interesting how the nurse's comment, "You don't look 83," made me feel better, for I feel haggard, ugly and old these days.

This morning I read, "Lay not up treasures that moth and rust consume," and I go on trying to increase my savings, that I may not be a burden in the time of illness. In my grandparents' day, they must have never worried about the financial costs of dying. The family doctor would come at a nominal fee and they would be cared for at home. Now we live too long and medicine and nursing care keep us alive far beyond our time.

God, I know these pratterings[sic!] are personal and self-centered, but my concern for each of my loved ones is deep. This summer was so helpful in every way and I was blessed by it all. Show me how to bless others.

I need to write many letters. I want them to be helpful, appreciative messages. Speak through me. Let me add to the supply of love and kindness in the world. People say my speeches were of worth to them, let the same be true of letters.

Mae

★ ★ ★

Dear God,

I had such a good night of sleep. Thank You. I sit here in perfect comfort . . . . What a blessing this place is. Why are we so blessed? How can I show my appreciation for the luxury? Things are not equal in this world. Some of us have so much more—I wish everybody could share in this.

. . . .

Another strange period of non-awareness in church this morning, when I didn't realize the offering was being taken. I heard the Scripture, but I did not see the deacons move off the platform or know when the plate was passed to me. I did know I needed to put in an offering for the building fund, so I had put $20 in an envelope with my name on it and was waiting to put it in the plate, when I realized the offering had been taken. I sat there stunned, with the thought of what had happened, and did not rise to sing the Doxology. God, *what* happened? What do I do when there is nothingness? How do I believe? What can be done to avoid this? *It is all so frightening.*

How unfortunate that the last memories people have of us have to be those of degeneration. What happens to the core, the heart, the soul of the person? Surely it does not shrivel and shrink to worthlessness. How do You stay with us, "all the years of my life," when the brain cells function in unpleasant ways?

I think of myself, God, as the run-of-the-garden variety Christian, but, this morning, I realized that, *maybe,* I had been given some of the attributes of real Christians, and people do see You in me. It is a marvelous and awesome thought! If I do, grant me *greater* humility.

Your servant,

Mae

★ ★ ★

★ ★ ★

Dear God,

I awoke today, saying, "I love living here." The mornings are mine, quiet, uninterrupted by anything outside the apartment. No phone calls, no knocks on the door. I love it. I am becoming a recluse. I am more selfish. I don't think this is the way You want me to move, God—at least it is not the way I have followed in the past. Because of my years, is it alright now? I do not have the energy, the desire, the will to do very much. If I should be doing more, Oh God, energize me to move.

My fears are big, my love for You is not big enough to overcome my fears. I understand Your love for me, but it will not necessarily do for me what *I* think is best. I want, with all my heart, to be able to place my hand in Yours. Can You help me do that? What law governs this relationship with You? My nights are full of thoughts of dying and dewath and I long to get it all over with. I feel the need to be useful by speaking, but now I am afraid to make the effort for fear of a seizure or a stroke. . . . .

This time the "black-out" was almost complete. Thank You that I came out of it in a few minutes. Guide me in the days to come.

Rolling Thunder said, "There is a way of thinking about these things so they won't be that way."* Do we have anything at all to say about the time of our death? Is the right to choose taken from us completely in this, when it isn't in other things? Do we instinctively hang onto life or can we do anything, one way or the other?

How can I show Your love today? What acts of kindness can I show? To whom should I write?

Mae

---

*ibid., p. 131.

★ ★ ★

Dear God,

Good morning. The clouds scurry across the skies. The wind blows. The house is quiet, save for the ticking of the clock. I am at peace, grateful for blessings too numerous to write. How do I express gratitude, so deep it hurts? In its efforts to burst its boundaries, my soul sings a psalm which has no words, for words (beautiful as they are) fail to express my feelings.

All around today, there are evidences of Your care and the love of others. Bill has just brought over his hose and has started the water running at the roots of the new red maple. Last night, Barbara threw her arms around me with, "I love you." Frances called from Indianapolis, "I wanted to hear your voice." Such events are like burning leaves that smolder when suddenly a flame comes alive and you know that within the smoldering leaves there is light and brightness . . . so with the surprise events of life, as widened by love.

Are You interested in what happened this morning? I found it so funny. They tried to show an interview with me on TV and there was no sound. It was so funny, looking at us talking away and hearing nothing. I got the giggles. Later, Bill came and threw his arms around me and said, "I'm sorry. I wouldn't have done that to you, of all people." It was sweet of him. If I had had a brother, I would have wanted one like Bill. Bless him and give him long years of health.

I record here, before You, that I had another slight stroke yesterday. It was frightening, but I recovered. My deep gratitude that I can write You this morning. I am so thankful that I can function. A year ago today, I was feeling badly and a few days later I blacked out and was in the hospital. God, do help me to put my trust in You. Grant to me peace, calmness, grace. Let not my heart be troubled. Let me now keep as quiet as possible and give Your Spirit time to work.

I look out my window and behold the gorgeous golden marigolds in my garden. As they gladden my heart with their beauty, help me to gladden others today. The Vietnamese girl is sweeping the bedroom now. Let Your grace fall on her.

Mae

Dear God,

You are in charge. I am more and more willing to say it that way. I am ceasing to pray about my manner of death, not saying, "Let me live until such and such a time or occasion," or "Let me die quickly." I have spent *too much* time at that, and because I believe You answer prayer, I have felt such prayers would influence what happened. I want to cease using time that way. *You are in charge and I am grateful!*

Thank You for an interesting night of dreams. Am I supposed to learn anything from them? That was such a wonderful train ride coming down a gorge, with fast-flowing water, passing people on donkeys waving banners, excited because the sight of the city would soon burst into view. Is this my life, going faster and faster, excited because the "City of God" will burst into view?

It takes so long to learn, God. Life is gone before we do.

Mae

★ ★ ★

Dear God,

I feel like "Cuddly Bear" today—with no spine to hold me up, needing to be propped up as he is on the couch. Prop me up, God, and help me through this day.

The wind has howled and screeched all night, fitting my mood of uncertainty. Something serious is wrong, or I would cease losing weight. I keep thinking of Kathleen and the way she faced death. Dear God, help me to do equally well to accept death calmly. You have helped me through so many experiences over the years, let Your strength and courage flow in me. Keep me remembering Your loving kindnesses of the past and continuing to give You praise for the many years of opportunities I have had. "You are in charge" has freed me from anxiety. Now, I want to release my will into "Thy will be done." I really do.

An old favorite found. How we loved Sara Teasdale in the '20s. Do You remember—

> This is the spot where I will lie
> When life has had enough of me,
> These are the grasses that will blow
> Above me like the living sea.
>
> These gay old lilies will not shrink
> To draw their life from death of mine.
> And I will give my body's fire
> To make blue flowers on this vine.
>
> "Oh Soul," I said, "have you no tears?
> Was not the body dear to you?"
> I heard my soul say carelessly,
> "The myrtle flowers will grow more blue."*

---

*"In A Burying Ground," from *Love Songs,* by Sara Teasdale. Macmillan Publishing Company, 1975.

I remember, so clearly, the myrtle beds beside the stone walk at 238 Ohmer . . . so many memories . . . A wonderfully full life has been given me, but now, God, I am weary beyond words.

Mae

★ ★ ★

Dear God,
I give thanks and affirmation for this letter of love from Don Jeff.
". . . You have shown me that valleys and mountains
are only the inverse of each other,

That the night always follows
yet calls forth the day,

That fear lies only
in the unknown,

That tears can end droughts
and that doing dispels despair,

That variety is at the
heart of creativity,

That being a 'servant'
is an invaluable perspective,

That, in giving,
we do truly receive,

And in dying to one another
we are born anew ourselves.

Thank you, Mother of mine."

Truly, I have been granted love unlimited!

Unlimited love.
Love knocked down
but never out.

Love with a black eye
but still smiling.

Love straightened up and
saying, "Let's try again."

Love stretching out her
arms and saying, "Come here, Honey."

Oh, God, welcome me, when I come.

Mae

The Last Entry

Dear God,

Here I am, Mae Ward.

I'm still on a pilgrimage.

I'm still in kindergarten, trying to handle the blocks of life and string the beads of prayer. To commune is still my goal, as difficult as that may be. Be patient and understanding of my hesitancy and my bumblings.

I read the saints and find they came to You directly. If You had not heard and answered, would not prayer have vanished from the face of the earth and the minds of men and women? "The only proof of prayer *is* prayer." That sounds so simplistic, certainly not sophisticated at all, but so is the reality of the air I breathe which gives me LIFE. PRAYER, like air—I'll bet my very life on it.

The pain in my shoulder and my arm—is it "God-sent"? No, I think not. It is the result of the years and the grown-old body. What a problem it is to handle. I know death is coming. It will be welcome if it can come fast, but the idea of a quick departure is such an obsession with me that handling a long, slow departure will be even harder. Grant to me a feeling of security that Your love and care abide, regardless of anything. That nothing, absolutely nothing, can separate us from Your love, Oh God. Gentle Jesus, let Your grace descend upon me.

My faith is as a candle, flickering in the dark . . .

Almost, but not quite, the wind of pain puts it out.

Almost, but not quite, the uncertainty of the future makes it flicker.

Almost, but not quite, unanswered prayers (unanswered according to my perceptions), cause the flame to struggle to keep burning.

"Mae, your faith is your salvation."

I'll keep trying, God. Have patience with me!

Good night, 'til we meet tomorrow,

Mae

★ ★ ★

Postscript

A long-distance call came from the doctor at the Kansas City hospital: "Your mother has just suffered a massive stroke. She has not regained consciousness. If she lives, there may be considerable paralysis and brain damage."

I sat stunned and sickened. Mae's greatest fear, lingering on in half-life, was now a possibility. Not for Mae, this stifling conclusion to a vital life. I prayed as I *knew* she would have me, that this cup would pass from her. Many times in our life together, I had seen what seemed to be miracles wrought by her prayers. I had known, first-hand, healings of body and rejuvenation of spirit. Now, it was her turn.

As I wept and prayed and reached out to her . . . I suddenly found myself kneeling by her bed. As she lay paralyzed, I looked on her and saw in her face no pain or fear. Taking her hand in mine, I whispered in her ear a phrase she had said many times, "Mae, let go and let God, let go and let God."

The phone jarred me. It was the doctor again. "I'm sorry. Your mother has just passed away. I can assure you, she did not suffer. She was very peaceful at the end." "I know," I responded, and thanked God that *our* prayer had been heard!

Rejoice!
Go forth with singing into a new day,
   For we have been shown once again that
   God dwells among us.
Rejoice!
   We have not lost Mae. She is not lost,
   for we know where she is, because we know
   who she was and we know Whom she knew.
Rejoice!